Wirt Gerrare

The Warstock

A Tale of to-morrow

Wirt Gerrare

The Warstock
A Tale of to-morrow

ISBN/EAN: 9783337071387

Printed in Europe, USA, Canada, Australia, Japan

Cover: Foto ©ninafisch / pixelio.de

More available books at **www.hansebooks.com**

THE WARSTOCK:

A TALE OF TO-MORROW.

BY

WIRT GERRARE,

LONDON.
W. W. GREENER.
1898.

DEDICATION

TO

J. N., H. G., & J. G. A.

Whose marvellous inventions in Mechanics and Chemistry have inspired this story.

AUTHOR'S PREFACE.

It is no longer the custom of writers of fiction to preface their books with an introduction. Where exceptions to this rule are made, more often than not the prefatory note consists merely of an apology for the story itself—therefore, is useless. In the present instance the writer is of opinion that the subject matter of his story is of that nature which renders some explanation desirable.

In the first place, THE WARSTOCK does not pretend to be Literature; it makes no appeal to the emotions, nor is it intended simply to amuse. Its purpose is to set intelligent people thinking; those persons who wish to deny their brains the exercise of this elementary function should read no further. The author wants neither their pence nor their attention, and values their plaudits as little as their sneers.

THE WARSTOCK purposes to be a story; a tale of that to-morrow when wireless telegraphy shall be general, and the use of explosives in war has been superseded; hence, it is a work of the imagination, not a controversial treatise on existing conditions. Nevertheless the incidents are based on certain facts, to some of which brief allusion may be made.

The most cursory examination of the history of the rise and progress of British industries will suffice to show that, in the combination of causes which wrought such a beneficial change in the fortune of Britain, the inventive genius of her manufacturers is the chief factor. The impetus given to her export trade by the creations of Arkwright, Compton, Dalton, Earnshaw, Hargreaves, and others has been maintained by the similar work of more recent inventors—on inventors Britain depends for continued progress.

It is notorious that at the present time no persons, as a class, are worse treated than inventors.

To the author it seems probable that inventors possess the intelligence to secure to themselves the full value of the property they create. This done, they will possess the power to rule which was assumed to be the prerogative of birth but is already actually in the command of the rich. It follows that with the substitution of riches for "noble-birth" as the criterion of worth, the creators of wealth will be regarded as the superiors of its mere possessors. The future, therefore, is for inventors.

At the present time, when inventors can scarcely obtain recognition of common rights, it seems idle to contend that nothing short of absolute supremacy will content them. But there is no good reason why they should ever be satisfied with less; and this is an age when, if progress can be made at all, it can be made quickly.

In a single year upwards of fifty thousand applications for "patents" are received at the British office alone—an absolute proof that the number of persons interested in inventions is immense. True, the majority of patents issued are for inventions of little value, or none, but of the true creative genius there is sufficient trace to indicate that, given suitable conditions, the higher order of invention would flourish. An examination of patent specifications will prove to what trivialities some great minds descend—even Lord Kelvin improved and patented the spigot of the common water-butt. Yet there are great inventions which have not been patented, and, in all probability, most of these never will be either protected—or made known. The men who discovered them are not novices in the science of invention, nor ignorant of the meaning and value of patent protection. Some earn their living by slight improvements to odds and ends—by some trifling alteration to the staple articles of trade. If present conditions continue, there is little doubt but the secrets of their chief discoveries will die with them.

The conditions which militate against the success of inventions of the highest order may be summarised. To the conditions imposed by legislation with respect to the granting of patents, the chief objection is that there is no real protection, or monopoly, conferred by a "patent"; while, on the other hand, the secret of the discoverer must be made known to all. Next, the time is too short;

fourteen years, the limit allowed, may be ample for the working of an invention applicable to some craze of the hour—say, a dress-holder to support the skirt or a walking-costume, for the trailing skirt may be gone for ever before next winter—but how if the invention be, say, a new mode of traction to supersede the steam locomotive? A good engine will work for thirty years, and, even if all railway companies were willing to adopt at once the new method, many years would elapse after the expiration of the longest patent before the invention could possibly attain its full value. If the invention referred to changes in the "permanent way," the patentee would have still fewer chances of obtaining early general exploitation of his invention. Then, the fees are too heavy; because out of proportion to the work done, or the benefit conferred. The initial fees cover all the expenses in connection with examination, registration, and storage of documents; out of the additional tax, in the shape of renewal fees, a costly free library is maintained and a handsome annual surplus goes to the Imperial Treasury. Foreign patent offices are also unfair to the inventor. A few years ago Mr. Edison calculated that if he had patented all his inventions in every country granting protection, he would have needed upwards of three millions sterling for the Government duties alone.

Legislation should assist and encourage inventors, rather than hinder them: vested interests and the innate conservatism of human nature are sufficiently powerful to effectually obstruct too rapid or undesirable progress. The inventor is usually considered to be a nuisance and mar-profit. A motor which would empty the engine-sheds at Crewe, Swindon, and Derby would not endear its inventor to the railway engineers; a process which would render obsolete the expensive plant of great steel works would not be run after at once by all the ironmasters.

But it is not my intention, either here or in the story, to dilate upon the rights and wrongs of patentees—the remedy for the hardships they endure is sufficiently obvious. If the many thousands who apply for patents are not satisfied with what is conferred, they are surely strong enough, if they make common action, to obtain such relief as legislation may afford. Doubtless patents are a prolific source of heartaches, and the least advance in the direction towards justice would make the term of protection date from the first commercial use of the invention, instead of from the date of the application for a patent. It is easy to picture some poor artisan with an invention of real utility to railway, gas, water, shipping, or other powerful corporations only—who can go on as they have done, and are doing; who prefer to do so rather than deal with the inventor, expecting that his poverty will prevent him paying the annual renewal fees, and that his invention will soon be available without payment by them. The man, hoping against hope, time after time scraping together the £10, or larger fee, for renewals, full of faith in his invention, enduring the jeers of his mates, bearing the rebukes of his wife when accusing him of starving his children for the worthless thing he has invented. Each year the tax becomes heavier, each year the man more obstinate; each year the invention loses value, and the possible users become less inclined to make terms. It needs not the novelist's imagination to supply the details of that picture. All know how the grim tragedy must end: few know how numerous such cases are.

Such subjects are not, I contend, most suitable for treatment by romancers; the reformer, the agitator, the practical philanthropist, the legislator—these may deal advantageously with actualities. If those who rule, in their wisdom, decide that inventive genius, like virtue, must be its own reward, the lot of the inventor may be as happy, but yet as unexciting, as that of the majority of righteous men and women whose lives are devoid of story.

To writers of romance, there are other aspects of invention offering greater attractions; notable among these the changes that must result from the exploitation of a truly great invention.

It is the inventor who will bring about the next great revolution in the world's history, and this truth I have attempted to make clear in THE WARSTOCK. As already hinted, inventions of great moment have been made, are still being made, and will continue to be made until, some day, from among the great scattered army of workers will arise the man to whom a really great invention will give the absolute mastery.

The nature of the invention and the character of the man are purely matters for speculation. In THE WARSTOCK I have given but fanciful sketches of persons and things—actual discoveries, revealed in confidence to me by inventors, are unlike, save in their newness, those I have instanced in story.

Another point: in that future when inventors rule, will there be a closer approximation to exact justice than now obtains?

The wonderful advance made during the century now reaching its end has been almost entirely upon the material plane. The rushing stream of progress appears to have forced morals into a backwater; at the close of the nineteenth century the English people have no clearer conception of justice than had their forefathers two centuries and a half ago; no greater love of liberty than their Scandinavian ancestors who, in search of untrammelled freedom, forced their clumsy viking ships over fearful and distant seas; no sterner sense of duty than possessed by the myriads who have struggled, and suffered, and died—for king, or faith, or kindred. To-day we possess no virtue that was unknown to our forefathers; not a vice they practised but disgraces our boasted civilisation. The paid gladiators of ancient Rome have their counterpart in the salaried football players of modern England; mediæval times had their Trade Guilds as these days have their Trade Unions.

This age excels those past only in the fields of discovery and construction—even in the highest arts it is only the execution that is better, there is no evidence of greater inspiration, no proof of higher ideals. Such excellence as there is, then, is not due to priest, or lawgiver, or warrior; has not resulted from the heart's yearning, the introspections of the metaphysician, the rhapsodies of the seer. It is the lowly toiler who, little by little, has wrested secrets from Nature, and learned fresh truths. It is the inventor who has extirpated the drudgery of toil from the lives of most, and can save from sheer physical labour both man and beast.

It is the inventor who has placed in the hands of those whom he has been taught to consider his superiors, the weapons which have given his effete rulers the mastery over him, as well as over the bravest barbarians and the craftiest of cultured foes. Is it too much to expect that the inventor has grown wary since the power he has entrusted to others has been grossly misused? Too much to expect, that some day a man will recognise that his invention, jealously guarded and fully exploited, will advance him to absolute supremacy?

WIRT GERRARE.

CONTENTS.

CHAP.		PAGE.
I.	Concerning an Interesting Discovery	1
II.	The Limitations of a Millionaire	7
III.	Aristocrats and an Isocrat	13
IV.	A Conversational Dance	24
V.	The First Move Forward	31
VI.	Concessions	39
VII.	In Cristallia	52
VIII.	A Renegade	62
IX.	Defences	66
X.	The Day Dreams of a Business Man	77
XI.	A Baptism of Fire	84
XII.	Knights of the Back-Stairs	94
XIII.	"For the Future of Cristallia"	100
XIV.	Unwelcome Visitors	109
XV.	A "Pot-Luck"	116
XVI.	Strange Idols	125
XVII.	A Predicament	131
XVIII.	The Privilege of the Minority	136
XIX.	Fortune Favours Cristallia	139
XX.	The Esoteric Section	144
XXI.	In the Conning-Tower	153
XXII.	Retaliation	159
XXIII.	Death	164
XXIV.	Flight	167
XXV.	The Soulless Avenger	177
XXVI.	Panic	184
XXVII.	The "Warstock" in Action	193
XXVIII.	"Foightin' Larry av the Guard"	201
XXIX.	The Last Struggle for Supremacy	209
XXX.	Conclusion	216

THE WARSTOCK.

CHAPTER I.

CONCERNING AN INTERESTING DISCOVERY.

AT last there was a record! This time there was no doubt. When Robert Sterry depressed the key of the transmitter the needle on the indicating dial suddenly responded; was yet vibrating appreciably.

Willie Redhead, watching the instrument from his invalid's chair, did not need to call Robert's attention to the success; no sooner had the inventor touched the key than he strode hastily across the laboratory and gazed earnestly at the register.

"I *felt* it was all right this time," he muttered.

"Try it again."

"No, no! Not now!"

"How you tremble! It's—it's all right. Unmistakably a record."

"We are on the verge of a vast thing, Willie."

"I know it. I know it—the greatest discovery of the century."

"Of all time," said Robert decisively.

The invalid said no more, but watched the inventor in moody silence passing rapidly to and fro. Full of vigour, hardly able to suppress his excitement, the boards creaked loudly beneath

B

Robert's feet and the invalid's chair shook until Willie Redhead could have shrieked with the pain the slight vibrations produced. There seemed no limit to the energy of the other, and Willie, unable to endure the agony longer, interrupted plaintively:

"Wheel me into the study, Bob."

"Forgive me! I forgot——"

"I understand. I want to think too. Is it very late?"

"I'm afraid it is. No, only just past midnight."

"You won't try it again? Just once?"

Robert Sterry shook his head: he felt like a boy who, after innumerable futile plashings, first succeeds in keeping his mouth above water, and not knowing whether by hands or feet he has accomplished so much, defers further essays to another day. On the other hand, Willie Redhead felt only the ecstasy that comes with the first feeble mastery of a new element, and desired further evidence of prowess. As soon as Robert had gone he rang for his man; wheeled back into the workroom, *he* now pressed the lever and saw the indicator respond, and repeated the experiment again and again until the tired servant could no longer keep his eyes open to note the revolutions of the needle on the dial.

Nature had fashioned Willie Redhead in the noblest mould; an accident in childhood, with careless nursing and clumsy surgery, rendered him a hopeless cripple. A line of long-dead ancestors had been vikings, and in him was implanted their love of the sea; he felt an uneasy craving for a wild life in conflict with the elements; pictured delight as being tempest-tossed in a cockle-shell of a boat, and glory in penetrating ice-bound regions no man had ever trod. Hoped for these delights and glories too, until one day, after battling long with surgeons' remedies, he was told that a cure was beyond reach. A weaker character would have succumbed at this cruel truth; the knowledge that though some day he might be better he could never be well, would never walk, with or without crutches, must never expect to be at ease or attempt physical exercise, only determined him to make the most of his vegetable-like existence. His sister Jessie cheered him on; he threw himself heart and soul into the study of physical science. The more abstruse the problem, the easier forgotten the ever-present bodily pain; and now he was rewarded as no man ever was, except Robert—and Robert too had suffered, but in another way.

The quest had been long and anxious, but to Willie, shut off from other pursuits, it had been pleasurable enough; the discovery of itself was ample reward for both, for they had found what others had long sought unsuccessfully. To call up at will a force of which none knew anything, and most denied even the existence, to play with it, to measure it, to dally with it, was to experience such bliss as none but inventors know.

Then with what joy they set about to master the unknown! With what pleasurable anticipation they noted the manifestation of the new force, presenting the most delicate lures perfected by science; anon, saving themselves as best they could when their instruments were shattered by the fierce strength of the erratic agent. All was not easy work, not even safe work; at times platinum wires suddenly fused without apparent cause; steel plates were shivered, blocks hurled against and through the walls, stanchions twisted, rafters broken. More than once operators and apparatus were thrown to the ground in a confused heap; twice the laboratory was set on fire; once, in quite broad daylight, it was inexplicably wrecked as completely as though crushed by a thunderbolt. But it was nothing to brave these and kindred dangers in exchange for the pleasure that accomplished ever so little supremacy over the unknown.

Robert Sterry had not looked so well since Jessie Redhead died as he did now; his light-heartedness did not return, and the mother knew she had lost her boy for ever, and fretted; but his father now found in him a comrade and took him into his confidence and disclosed some part of his vast wealth, thinking thereby to entice the lad from laboratory investigations to commence his work in the management of money and the acquisition of more, which is the millionaire's lifelong task. Young Robert listened, but was not tempted; his talk was of isomers as often as his father's was of dollars. The power of money was a form of energy he could not comprehend since it could not be expressed either in thermal units or in watts. He heeded all that was said, but his thoughts and his hours were mostly devoted to the development of the "Sterrygraph" — for so Redhead insisted upon naming the new transmitter.

Little by little the experimenters learned the nature of the poltergeist with which they were dealing, and at once essayed to harness the new power to the service of man. Any deflection of the needle now, made at will, produced a corresponding vibration of the indicating needle; they had only to obtain the same action irrespective of distance and earth telegraphy, and the transmission of messages without the aid of wires would be an accomplished fact. It would be a practical application of their invention; acceptable, needed; and towards its achievement they worked unceasingly.

"Have you thought what this invention means to us, Willie?"

"It will take us to the very front," answered the cripple proudly, for he was ambitious.

That was before they discovered their limitations; they were young and sanguine, and no man who has wrested the most trifling secret from Nature but is confident in his own might.

Further experiments somewhat subdued their expectations; but as a telegraph the invention was efficient; this, tests proved conclusively. Robert travelled about alone with his transmitter; far and near on the American continent he made the earth contact and communicated with Willie Redhead in the invalid's chair at the Plainfield laboratory. It was a wonderful performance, and the secret of its production was still their own.

On one of these journeys Robert was notified of his father's death. Returning home, the wealth to which he was heir staggered him by its magnitude. He felt crushed beneath the weight of dollars, for he saw that they would prove a nuisance—that he would be expected to live for them instead of for the one thing for which he really cared, the invention that was his and Willie Redhead's. Comprehending this, he at once determined to be the master instead of the slave of his wealth. At present he had no need of money for any purpose, and, remembering what his father had said as to its employment, put the dollars away safely for a time and tried to forget them.

"The Sterrygraph" was made complete; when it was workable, a perfect instrument for the purpose intended, the inventors felt that the time had come to make its advantages known and reap the harvest for which they had tilled and sown.

They expected some opposition; a million and a half miles of telegraphic cable enclose the earth like a network. These cables and wires would be unnecessary and valueless when the "Sterrygraph" was adopted, and those interested in the threatened property would combine to crush the newcomer out of existence. In America alone such a combination could command many more million dollars than Sterry had; so to be successful, the "Sterrygraph" would need to be exploited for all it was worth. The inventors never doubted that its money value, however great, would not be readily obtainable. They wanted more; the "Sterrygraph" was, in their estimation, a very great thing; it would bring fame and honour to them if only properly introduced. As Robert said,

"Never was Yankee born or bred
"Without that peculiar kink in his head
"By which he could turn the smallest amount
"Of whatever he had to the best account."

and, believing this, they intended to take the world by storm. Nothing that could be done in America would be worth doing unless Europe fell into line, and to Europe straightway went Sterry with his crippled friend.

CHAPTER II.

THE LIMITATIONS OF A MILLIONAIRE.

NEWSPAPER correspondents hunted long and assiduously for Robert Sterry; when the representative of a New York journal discovered the young millionaire in Paris, he slily watched him sip a cup of coffee, then promptly cabled over a long account of the way the American was passing his time in the gay city. The next day the account, with additions, found its way back to Europe as news.

Robert Sterry was fresh to the cruel glare of publicity; offensive to his nature at any time, he found it particularly so when he was endeavouring to negotiate his invention with a governmental department. Hoping to escape the interviewer, he hurried to London; at one of the monster hotels favoured by his countrymen he fancied he could hide his identity and, like hundreds of other guests, become simply a number.

He sat among strangers at the large table and once again ate his dinner unnoticed. For a time he had dodged the great limelight of the Press, only to learn that no shade is dense enough to long screen the millionaire. "The Pimlico Gazette," the organ of high cookery and smart society, had devoted a wide column of smallest type to chronicle his commonplace behaviour at Paris, and now, unrecognised, he found himself the topic of conversation.

A sturdy Briton objected to newspaper space being occupied by twaddle concerning a simple monied man. An American retorted that in Europe newspapers, like everything else, were small, and what space they had was wanted to set forth the still less important doings of the merely titled. Then Robert Sterry heard that millionaires were the aristocrats of America, as indigenous to the United States as Baronets were to Britain or Princes to Poland; and that in the popular estimation the millionaires of the world ranked next to ruling sovereigns.

"Vulgar money-worship," sneered the Briton.

"All are born; but not every one born even to a dukedom can make money."

"Some are born to titles; others only to dollars; most to neither one nor the other."

"Quite so, and those born to titles seldom win more; those born to wealth win other things; consequently the career of a millionaire is more important than that of a landlord. Your greatest estates are all entailed; the tenants know what to look forward to—whether he be a 'good' landlord or a 'bad' one is all they wish to know respecting the successor in title, for from former experiences of both kinds they knew well enough what to expect. No one can tell what the millionaire will do with his money."

"All have soon found their limitations," growled the Briton.

"Agreed, agreed—but will the others? Will this Robert Sterry, for instance? His father was busy all his life making money, but the young man knew nothing of the wealth, or its immense power. He was brought up as his father had been, a simple working man. Now he has twenty millions of dollars at least; suppose he finds a new fulcrum on which to rest the lever of his wealth, as some one certainly will some day, and instead of frittering away time and money in the manner of a British aristocrat, determines upon some revolutionary scheme?"

"Unlikely. Wealth depends upon existing conditions being maintained, so millionaires are the very last persons to do anything revolutionary."

"These young men have no traditions behind them. Old Bob Sterry was a furnace-man; his son may have ideas. What ideas? That is just what we want to know, and that is why everything about him interests us."

"Well, what are his ideas?" asked the Briton contemptuously.

The American seemed well informed; he was sure young Sterry would do something unexpected of him or any other millionaire; lead a revolution or found a monastery—anything. He said that he had known his father intimately, and repeated often-heard stories of "Honest Bob," the terror of Wall Street: how in his youth he had emigrated from the Tyneside with nothing but a glassblower's pipe and tongs; how his wife tramped the townships in the swamps of Illinois harnessed to heavy baskets and carrying a child on each arm while hawking the fragile wares her husband so deftly fashioned; how, after thirty years at the blowpipe, his lungs gave way, and he had to sell to others the colours he knew how to make for himself, and how he grew rich thereby; the uses he made of his money, and how his luck never forsook him; yes, even the present Minister of the United States to the Court of St. James's would gladly own that he was indebted to "Honest Bob" for a good turn when he was being cruelly squeezed by Wall Street "bears." Robert listened to it all patiently, but without much interest; the man knew so much of his intimate affairs that he expected him to speak of the mysterious laboratory work and his great discovery, but his countryman either knew nothing or did not think either matter worth mentioning. Instead, he talked of Robert's attachment to Jessie Redhead, and at the first mention of her name Robert left the table.

But the journalist had effectively labelled him with his father's millions; even the six-foot-six embodiment of consequence who watched the hall door now recognised the docket, and attended with unwonted deference and alacrity to his order for a hansom. The cringing servility of one seemingly so great did not flatter; he took it as a reminder that the man Robert Sterry was becoming wholly hidden from the view of his fellows by the glittering tinsel of wealth it was his fortune to support.

The cab took him to a small ugly villa at Fulham; there, in a large room on the ground floor, sat Willie Redhead amid the books, charts, and instruments to which he was accustomed at Plainfield.

"What cheer, Willie!"

"You back so soon. Have you——"

"No; nothing done. It is only waste of time to try the postal departments; telegraphic messages have always been sent over wires, and that way they shall go until empires fall."

"But they will have to take it."

"Of course. Meanwhile, Germany refuses, Austria declines, Russia demurs, Italy has no intention of making any change, France is not prepared to entertain any proposal—and here?"

"We have not got beyond the exchange of polite pourparlers."

"And never will. It is their way. We are not wanted, Willie, neither is our invention; that is the truth."

"Yet it was to carry us to the very front."

"So it will; so it shall! First we must make a way for it. No such molehill of a difficulty as a little official obstruction shall stop us, I warrant you. If conventional methods fail, we will try others. Where is my mail?"

Willie Redhead pointed to a huge pile of letters.
"All those?"

"I suppose it's Warren's doing."

"That confounded article in the 'Matin,' I expect. Any callers?"

"Quite an army to-day. Warren says you must be sure to go to the Countess Kyrwick's to-night. I did not think you would be back; you'll see the card somewhere there. It is a big affair; a lot of influential people sure to be there, Warren told me.'

"What sort of people?"

"Oh, Royalties, and Branson, and Fitzjoy——"

"The confounded Jack-in-office who referred me to the sub-assistant to the under-superintendent of the Construction Inspecting Department? Thanks! I'll go."

"Try him again?"

"What else for to-night?"

"Mrs. Deadwater, Mr. Justice James, Mrs. Spoor——"

"I'll go there too; old friends of your people, aren't they? Who is Feyda Vetini?"

"Not know Feyda Vetini? The world-renowned prima donna! Such is fame! I am ashamed of you. You are almost as ignorant of what every one knows as the average British Judge. She called—and what a voice!"

"What did she want? Millions, I suppose?"

Redhead nodded. "And you, of course. She was somewhat brusque and rude to me, but her voice was——"

"Bother her voice! What was she like to look at?"

"Small, lithe, not insignificant. Jewish type of face. But her voice——"

"H'm! Who else?"

"A Captain Tomes to sell you 'The Daily Express'; Lord Sines to propose you for the Amphitryon; half a dozen job-masters; a score of house-agents; two hundred tradesmen's cards; of begging letters and of circulars a thousand, more or less; and—and—oh, a man with a pedigree bloodhound."

"I'm not going to start a menagerie nor yet run an office to answer letters."

"Insert an advertisement in 'The Times' to the effect that the enquiries of all unknown correspondents will be answered by the 'Sterrygraph' when adopted by the British Government."

"That would be putting them off to the Greek Kalends politely. Anything more to hand?"

"Yes, the calculating machine. You see I am at work already."

"Capital. I wish you would let me help you."

He looked wistfully at a large chart showing the curves of equal magnetic variation for the year 1895, and then to the boxed-up Arithmometer before Redhead.

"It is my only privilege. I shall have the indices ready by the time you have won over the public. How we arrive at the key is to be kept secret too, remember."

"You are sure it does not pain you to twist that crank round so much?"

"Not at all. I want no assistance."

"I do. I wish this work done, and we free to return to our experiments."

"We do not invent solely for our own amusement, Bob. You go to the Countess Kyrwick, now!"

"You, too, know the limitations of a millionaire!"

CHAPTER III.

ARISTOCRATS AND AN ISOCRAT.

THERE could be no doubt as to the importance society attributed to the Countess Kyrwick's soirée. The hall was thronged when Robert Sterry arrived; he had some difficulty in getting to the stairs, when halfway up the passage became blocked; no moving up or down, right or left, and there he remained for three parts of an hour in unpleasant proximity to a stout Jewess and a burly admiral. Immediately before him, on the arm of a Privy Councillor, was the most generally admired fashionable beauty and amateur society journalist. They seemed the most interesting people in his immediate neighbourhood. He could hear their conversation distinctly above the hubbub of talk and smothered laughter. She objected to the glaring colours of the National Flag; declared the grimy houses of gray London were made still more hideous by the window-boxes of gay calceolarias, pelargonium, and lobelia; in her opinion ox-eye daisies and mignonette alone were permissible —in this taking her cue from the sentiment of the favourite society poet who could hear the talk, being ten stairs higher, but could not bend his head to see his "loved Lady Laureate." She pointed him out to her companion, and Robert thought how the glossy bald head firm held by the inordinately high collar resembled a huge billiard ball fast in a lathe chuck. This fancy took his thought to Willie, laboriously, painfully, but joyously grinding away at the Arithmometer crank in his lone den, while he himself, still more lonely in this throng, was frittering away his time ingloriously. He then became critical; noticed that although the men were of every size and age, the women for the most part were apparently young. All wore red-gold wigs of precisely the same pattern; of one cut too their dresses, aping each other even in the variety of aniline dye with which they were stained; all adopting the same pose; one and all marked to the same extent by the artificial blush on each cheek; of one sort their voices and their words.

He read next day that the throng was fashionable and brilliant; to him all seemed idle, decaying, ghastly. His technical training had spoiled his appreciation for such application of art. Beauty he could not see; he easily recognised bismuth and rouge, dead hair and peroxide of hydrogen, while the all-pervading odour of ambergris was loathsome and stifling.

As he stood there, the continuous idle chatter, stifled laughter, mock smiles, the very inertness of the mass of humanity surrounding him, forced him to the conclusion that from such as they he could extract nothing that would advance his work.

At last there seemed to be a movement onward; the throng swayed, but that was all—except that a few more crowded from the hall on to the bottom stair, and the pressure was greater than before.

"I fear the Prince will have gone," sighed the lady journalist.

"What matters that if the new millionaire remains?" cynically observed the Privy Councillor.

"Millionaires are so common nowadays."

"That is ambiguous."

"Construe it in either sense—it is correct."

"You may think otherwise later."

"Is this one of the American or African variety?"

ARISTOCRATS AND AN ISOCRAT.

"American, I believe."
"Of the two sorts the more detestable. His name?"
"Jerry, or Berry, or Sterry."
"Pray be precise; one must know his name at least."
"Robert Sterry, then."
"How plebeian! Of Chicago?"
"Of Plainfield, New Jersey."
"That sounds agrarian. Is he really wealthy?"
"A billionaire."
"In dollars?"
"Of course. By-the-bye, I heard a funny story about him to-day."
"Really good?"
"Very."
"Then not to his credit."
"Quite the reverse. Three years ago——" His voice sank to a whisper, but still Robert could hear every word.
"Excuse me, but my name is Robert Sterry."
He spoke low, but something in the intonation made each syllable heard throughout the hall, and there was an instant silence, followed by a rustle of silk as people turned to look towards the speaker.

The Privy Councillor turned too and bowed. The lady journalist alone was unmoved.

"How provoking! I believe that for once you were going to say something of interest."

"Really, that is too bad," laughed the Privy Councillor.

"I shall ask you to tell me later," she said; then turning, with a comprehensive gaze looked at, all around, and past Robert, who felt confused, and feared he had done amiss.

He could not understand such manners; he was better used to the ways of straightforward men and women, and longed for the whirr of the belting, the ringing laughter and glad songs of the factory girls, the cheery whistle of the toilers. He tried to picture such as they on the stairs, and these people dodging belts and pulleys, standing in the glare of the furnace or stooping over the anvil; he saw that the toilers would be men and women still, whatever the garb they wore, but of the people around him he could make nothing but puppets.

Suddenly the crowd surged forward; there was nothing to stay its progress. Soon Robert had escaped the stairs, passed through a grand reception-room en suite to the ballroom beyond. There was space for all. By-and-bye he was noticed; people dodged here and there before him; he was introduced first to one, then to another, until he was quite bewildered. The ponderous Jewess by whose side he had stood in silence for an hour was now all smiles and volubility; a Miss Betham was anxious to show him her ponies and drive him to Hurlingham; Lord Sines talked loudly of clam juice; the Hon. Stanbury Tisley wanted advice about Reading Rails; Branson invited him to pass into the smoke-room and hear the latest story. Dozens of women were brought to him since he could not be induced to move freely in the thronged room; their names were mentioned, they bowed, smiled, and retired to make room for others—even the lady journalist came face to face with him and did as the others had done. About them all was a sameness: in their faces, their conduct, their words, even in their titles they were alike; the proceeding became monotonous and wearisome. Robert found it ridiculous. Confused and bored, he was trying to escape when he met the Hon. Benjamin Blanchard Fitzjoy.

"O Sterry, glad to find you have forsaken that foolish invention for rational amusement."

"But I have not. I am coming to see you at the office to-morrow."

"Spare yourself the trouble, my good fellow; I have not yet heard from that—that——"

ARISTOCRATS AND AN ISOCRAT. 17

"Sub-assistant to the under-superintendent of the Construction Inspecting Department?"

"Yes, yes; Beers, that's his name. When I get his report I will communicate——"

"You will never get it unless——"

"Eh, haven't you——"

"No. I offered you the chance of introducing it; if you do not care to, I shall go higher, not lower."

"H'm! Really, what does it matter? Come and see me whenever you like, but don't talk shop now; I get too much of it in the House. Have you seen the Prince?"

Sterry shook his head.

"You do not mean to say you were—but of course you do not understand our ways yet. You should have come in by the other door and avoided that wait, but perhaps you—— Ah well, the Prince is in the supper-room now, or I would——"

"I wish you would introduce me to our host, or the Countess."

"Of course I will. Where are they? Oh, I see he is talking to the Princess; we must wait a minute or two. The fact is, there has been a slight hitch to-night. Feyda Vetini was expected an hour ago. She is to sing that new thing of Verdi's—no one has heard it yet. But she is not here—just like her. Hullo! there's Bardsey! I'll bet she's come now. Lord Bardsey is her particular friend at present, you know. But she will not come upstairs yet. Not she! Now, Sterry, if you will accept a moderate stake and lay long odds, I will take you that Feyda insists upon Kyrwick going downstairs to receive her, and that he will go. What do you say? Is it done for a pony at ten to one?"

Sterry shook his head.

"You would have lost. See, there he goes! I wonder if she has brought Monsieur Ducamel with her."

"Who is he?"

C

"Her son, of course. She takes him everywhere now."

"Hush! *Someone* may overhear us."

"The Princess? Not the least chance. Don't you know she is half deaf? Not altogether a disadvantage. She might often hear too much. Feyda delights in shocking the proprieties."

"I thought the Princess very popular."

"With the bourgeoisie she is. It is so easy to be esteemed by the lower orders. They will worship the very ground on which one treads if one be but moderately good and dull like themselves. The most difficult thing nowadays is to be irretrievably bad without intentional striving after wickedness. The Princess is an absolute and hopeless failure!"

"Delighted to hear you say so."

"But I should say millionaires have a good chance of succeeding. If money be the root of all evil, you know, then a plentiful crop of wickedness might grow naturally. I envy you your luck. She comes! She comes! Look at her, the bitch!"

A lane had opened in the throng, and along it came Earl Kyrwick, with all courtly grace conducting a slim, sallow-complexioned little woman of forty-five. A wisp of hair, towsled like a thrum mop, was thickly studded with diamonds, and fell in cunning disorder about a scraggy neck and features markedly Jewish. A wondrously draped loose robe, freely besprinkled with jewels and heavily fringed, alternately hid and revealed each line of her supple figure, in its every movement feline. Emeralds, diamonds, rubies sparkled upon her bosom; her fingers were almost wholly hidden by rings. She proceeded leisurely up the room to the orchestra; the Prince entered hurriedly and acknowledged her. Of intensely nervous temperament, and self-conscious to the finger-tips, she yet looked as unconcerned as a sphinx.

She spoke in French—of a sort, slurring her words

like an Israelite, yet commanding the admiration of all. With her rendering of Verdi's new music she said that she was not satisfied, neither could they be. She had a greater surprise in store for them; she would sing to them in English. Her voice thrilled them; they forgot the delay, for which she had not even apologised, they were delighted; in their aristocratic way they applauded warmly. Then very low came the strains of a well-known melody. In broken English and absolute silence the prima donna sang "Home, Sweet Home." In a few minutes she had finished, and was applauded. She felt tired, she said, and trusted they would not ask her to do more that night—an announcement which was less warmly received. Then Lord Bardsey hastily led her away to the supper-room.

"Bravo, Feyda, bravo! Excellent! Was ever such charming insouciance?" And Fitzjoy looked enquiringly at Robert.

"I should call it by another name," said Robert sternly.

The Under Secretary of State assumed his official attitude, screwed his monocle into his face, and asked abruptly:

"What?"

"Abominable insolence!"

The eyeglass fell, and a smile spread over the young man's features.

"Not really?"

"Why not?"

"Never state the obvious in common terms. It is bad art. Remember that golden rule—it will be worth more to you than millions in cash. But there's Sefton—must go—see you at Ancaster's on Friday.'

Passing through the crowd, Sterry heard many comments; for one who blamed the singer three were ready to praise her; some urged in extenuation that because the people of the Potteries had forced an encore from Patti the week before, Feyda thought it would be appreciated—at any rate she was bound to try; and so on, and so on. He found all this most uninteresting, and purchased his escape by the back stairs. Passing the supper-room door, he heard the singer complaining vehemently to Bardsey of her treatment; she saw Sterry, and called out loudly to him, but he heeded her not, and, once outside, determined never to enter the house again.

Clearly he had commenced too high in the social scale; from such people he could expect no help worth having. He drove to Bayswater.

Mrs. Spoor's "at-home" was a less important social function than the Countess Kyrwick's "reception"—yet in essentials the entertainment was the same. An exact observer, Robert noticed that the band played the same airs; there was a French singer from the same operatic company to which Feyda belonged. The hall and stairs were thronged, but not crowded; the house was more brilliantly illuminated; the dresses were not all of the same pattern or colour—some even contrasted gloriously with the sober livery of the footmen. In the reception-room a few energetic ones were waltzing; conversation was brisk; in all a suggestion of gaiety, which an occasional merry peal of laughter from some dim alcove or secluded corner confirmed.

He passed through the throng unnoticed and unrecognised; a stranger to his hostess, she welcomed him effusively—"it was so very good of him to come"; before he could assure her the obligation was his, she had abruptly left him. He wandered among the company, knowing no one, cut off from all.

They were people of a different class from those at the Countess's. These showed some individuality, a few even evidenced character which conventionality had failed to obliterate or recast; one or two robust men there were who looked fit and able to go anywhere and dare anything, as many women certainly brave enough to accompany them; but for the moment all sought amusement, and most seemed successful.

Robert quickly remarked one woman, like himself a stranger to the others. Young but not girlish, she was commonplace of figure and dress, passing to and fro unobtrusively. Her face interesting but not pretty, though her features were regular and good; the broad, high, even brow gave it its character—unmistakably intellectual. The eyes were hazel and well set, but the lashes and eyebrows faint to indistinctness; the cheeks pale, the lips bloodless but nervous; the mouth very mobile, with playful lines at the corners betraying the humour latent behind the demure mask of self-possession. The hair fair, fine, and abundant, almost ashen in its paleness, worn in massive plaits pinned closely to her head, undecorated with aigrette or jewel; fingers without rings, the sole trinkets a small scroll clasp and a watchchain neat to scantiness—a woman who disdained all decoration. In the hands of an adept maid well skilled in the arts of the Court costumer and theatrical "maker-up," the almost endless possibilities of figure, carriage, and pose would have been used to make this perplexing creature the most attractive woman in the company; instead, she was the most peculiar and least noticed of all—an excellent example of the latest modern type, a clever woman too, perhaps; beyond all doubt scholarly.

He was wondering how to obtain an introduction when a distinguished-looking old lady came up and addressed her as Miss Winship. She answered slowly, betraying by the slightest suspicion of sing-song in her speech that her home had been on the Tyneside; and this set Robert thinking. A few minutes later she was again alone on the landing leaning over the balustrade looking down into the hall.

"Miss Winship, I believe you have heard of me. I am Robert Sterry, of Plainfield, New Jersey. I heard of you through Jessie Redhead."

"The Redheads were friends of ours; I think I remember them staying with us at Shields some years ago, when they were on a visit to Europe. But you——"

"I am a great friend of her brother's—the cripple, you remember. He is with me in England now."

"Ah yes, I recollect something now; and what do you think of this country?"

"You are more than half American, I declare. This is my first visit, and I have not seen enough to warrant me in stating an opinion."

"That is quite English. Do you know many people here?"

"Only Mrs. Spoor; and she seems fully occupied. Do you find it dull?"

"Yes, and no. I came because Lady Reid wished it. She is one of the Governors of our school—I am a teacher in a High School for Girls at Kensington, you know, and I could not refuse. In a sense it is enjoyable, but frivolous. What do you think?"

"What will you think of me when I tell you it is the second to which I have been to-night. I left the Countess Kyrwick's but an hour ago."

"That, of course, was a very different gathering; it is the house of the smartest set in London! Why did you not stay?"

"Because it was the most deadly dull affair I ever visited. For liveliness even a White House reception could give it points and beat it."

"You have the American aversion to aristocrats."

"I am afraid it will end that way."

"As is only natural to a born democrat."

"To speak strictly I am a Republican. May I ask what you are?"

"I? Oh, I am an 'isocrat.'"

ARISTOCRATS AND AN ISOCRAT.   23

"Whatever is that?"

"An isocrat is a member of a society composed of people who take a serious view of life." And she laughed.

"It must be an order new to London."

"You must not judge us all by Lady Kyrwick's standard. Come and see us for yourself: we have an open meeting for recreation to-morrow evening, at Mrs. Smith's, The Boltons. You will find something quite different from this, and we are always ready to proselytise, though I may add we are all quite harmless. Shall I expect you?"

"Certainly you may."

"Now let me introduce you to Lady Reid. Whoever is that looking this way? See, he has recognised you, and gone straight off to Mrs. Spoor."

Sterry looked across the room and saw his hostess bustling towards them. She bowed graciously and took him by the hand.

"My *dear* Mr. Sterry, I must apologise! I really did not know you were Mr. Sterry—not *the* Mr. Sterry, you know. How could I have been so forgetful! Do let me introduce Captain Sibthorp. Captain Sibthorp — Mr. Sterry, of Connecticut. Where did you leave Lady Frere, Captain? Don't move from here, please, until I return. Where can she be?"

Several times Sterry tried to speak again with Miss Winship, but Mrs. Spoor, having discovered him, was not inclined to loose him into the hands of strangers. She gave him no rest until he "knew" all her set, and as he was hurried and harried he was conscious all the time of two mischievous eyes watching him amusedly, and the undisguised smile of merriment he saw playing about a pair of pale thin lips made him wish again and again that he had stayed on at Lady Kyrwick's. Never had he felt so ridiculous.

CHAPTER IV.

A CONVERSATIONAL DANCE.

THE next morning Robert called on the American Minister. He had a favour to ask. No, it was not the Prince of Wales's Levée; but if the representative of the United States would introduce him to some member of the British Government higher in rank than an Under Secretary of State, and preferably one whose foible was physics or science, then Sterry would feel under a lasting obligation."

"Why not the Duke of Hallamshire?"

"Never heard of him; I don't care whether it be the Prime Minister or simply Golden Stick in Waiting at the Back Stairs, if only he can tell a 'fast-speed-repeater' from the common 'sounder.'"

"I will see what I can do."

"To-day?"

"To-day or to-morrow."

Then he went straightway to his agent in the City, and at his instigation spent the rest of the day in calling upon "influential" people. These asked him to dinner, to lunch, or to liquor. They gave him a lot of advice, but no encouragement. An invention such as he described was not wanted at all. He grew disheartened; found the mountain of conventionality a formidable obstacle by no means easy to climb high enough even for a clear view of its extent. Every one expressed surprise that a man of his wealth should have nothing better to do than exploit a trivial invention—other ways of making money and fame were so much easier; but then, although they knew him to be a millionaire, they all seemed to think he must be hungry, or at least thirsty, so he did not think highly of their judgment.

He dined with Willie Redhead off a tough overdone steak and half-boiled potatoes, and his story was as unpalatable to his sanguine companion as was the spoiled food to himself.

"Who has called to-day?" he asked, wishing to change the topic.

"The same people, with one exception. Signora Vetini did not come."

"No one fresh?"

"A Lord Bardsey; he wished to see you at once. I sent him after you into the City. What do you do to-morrow?"

"Much the same thing. To-night, however, I am going to enjoy myself, and no one shall say me nay. I am going to work with you."

Then he remembered his promise to Miss Winship, and wished he had not spoken so hastily. He would have to go; but all the same he sat long talking with Willie.

It was late when he arrived at The Boltons. An elderly maidservant answered his ring, and entering the hall, a buzz of conversation from the room adjoining augured a lively time.

He was met by a tall, thin, figureless girl in a nondescript yellow dress. Her face was spoiled by a too large nose and an immense long fringe of straight tawny hair, the remnant of which was gathered up loosely into a small but most aggressive knot poised on the very apex of her crown. She had a large tortoiseshell fan dangling by a cord of golden silk from her wrist, several programmes in her hand, and she was throbbing with suppressed energy like a locomotive boiler under 200 lb. of steam.

"Mr. Sterry! *Salve!* Madeline told me to

expect you. I am the secretary, Hilda Kewney. Here is a programme. Shall I explain?"

"Please do," said Sterry, bewildered by the cardboard, headed with a mystical figure and bearing the legend: "Om mani padmi Aum."

"It is quite simple. Instead of dancing you talk. We are now at number three. That is a round dance, you see. For a round dance you choose your partner, go where you like, and until the M.C. tinkles his bell you debate the question. At present they are arguing 'Whether the primal curse be not a blessing in disguise.' If you take the affirmative you commence. You have only a few minutes in which to state your case and listen to your opponent refute it; therefore do not waste words. If you take the negative, it is best to let your partner do the talking, and demolish the last argument with an epigram—if you can. That is my way, and sometimes it is telling; I am standing out because I really do not know whether we ought to be gratified for labour or not; but I may say it is about the only topic on the programme I am not prepared to debate, taking either side. Always excepting Professor von der Pfordten's subject. You see that is a pas seul, and so it does not matter. For about five minutes we shall all listen while he demonstrates 'The Parallelogram of Forces exemplified in the Flight of a Boomerang.' I am not quite sure the good man knows what a boomerang is, but that is only a detail; he is certain to prove amusing, and probably instructive. Can I explain anything else?"

"A pas de quatre is a debate of four, of course; but what is a country dance?"

"Just a general talk. You can sit on either the affirmative or negative side; you, of course, do not need to be warned that to be counted with the majority is not necessarily to have the best of the argument. A skirt dance is for the ladies alone. The gentlemen will listen while we discuss 'The

A CONVERSATIONAL DANCE. 27

Weaknesses Inherent in Male Character.' You have your turn with 'The Un-reason of the Feminine Intelligence,' and I wish you well with your subject. We join forces again with the last item: 'Perfect Truth is Compatible with Good Manners.' That brings us to the end of the programme. 'The Envoy,' you see, is 'Be good, do good, not from fear of punishment or a hope of reward, but because it is good.' *That* you are expected to act up to during the whole course of your natural life. Now I think you know as much as I can tell you. I will give you a hint: do not monopolise the conversation. If you do, when next you ask the favour of a chat you may be shown the back of the programme. That means refusal—no rudeness is intended; it is merely woman exercising her prerogative. There is no obligation for you to invite every one or any one, but you are expected to do so."

"Then may I have the pleasure, Miss Kewney?"

"No. But I will not show you the back. There! You see it is full—and we have no extras. I am very popular when this game is played; if I do not talk as well as some of the others, I at least say as much. You *must* keep the conversation going merrily."

"I am an excellent and delighted listener."

"Really? Well, we have still five minutes. I will put you to the test. Come this way, and I'll show you the company through the other doorway, then you will not feel quite strange. You see there, by the conservatory, that long-faced young man is Boyd Robson, the son of the great railway contractor; he is a genius of a peculiar sort. The lady with whom he is talking is Edith Waters, the lady gymnast. Madeline Winship has her back towards us; Tom Spikens is listening to her—stupid fellow, why doesn't he talk? That is von der Pfordten on their left, with Mrs. Smith; Henry Toller is next; then Fred Stephens, the Theosophist, and Jennie Marion; Will Firbank next—we cannot see with whom he is talking. Young Carr, who writes sonnets, is with Alice Clowes here on my left; next Minnie Smith and John Buckley; Iltyd Jones, the inventor, with Ada Herbert, the black and white artist; and last Alan Winship, the assistant editor of 'The Industrial Weekly,' with Beatrice Tyacke. We cannot see those in the other part of the room, and some are in the conservatory; I'll introduce them to you later."

"I do not think you said who the young lady in red is—the one by the door?"

"You mean the one with the golden hair? Isn't it lovely? I thought you would notice her; do you not think her very beautiful, now? Some think her doll-like, but they do not know her. Who but she could wear carmine and not seem hideous? Now, I belong to half a dozen societies, and in none but this is there a really pretty girl to be found."

"The Isocrats are to be complimented."

"All are very proud of that particular member, I assure you. You see, very handsome girls do not usually venture into any society where anything of real interest is likely to be broached—it might attract attention from them, you know."

"They are wise, then, in their generation. But you have not told me her name?"

"Do you really wish to know? There goes the M.C.'s bell; I can do better now; I will introduce you. Come along! Mr. Robert Sterry—Miss Mavis Weyland."

The game went merrily, and Sterry fought through the programme conscientiously. The men held fairly to the rules of the debate, the ladies were a law unto themselves. They were not often academic, but terribly in earnest; assumed the side they took must be in the right and thus became wearingly didactic, sheltered themselves behind unassailable aphorisms, and fired the contents of technical treatises at their opponents. Occasionally they were original, more often bizarre; Madeline Winship told him, "Goodness is wholly a question of diet; if you underfeed you get crime, if you overfeed you beget vice." Beatrice Tyacke, an intense young person who seemed barely able to support the burden of existence because she was so awed by the immensity of its possibilities, somewhat astonished him by declaring that "beauty is only a concept, and the canons of art rest on a utilitarian base. Whatever form habit has made familiar and proved most suitable for the use intended to be made of it *is* beautiful."

"A chimney-stack?" ventured Sterry.

"Is certainly beautiful if undecorated; everything really of use when reduced by art and experience to its simplest form must be beautiful. That is an axiom. If you do not recognise it as beautiful, the fault is in your taste."

"The beauties of natural scenery, then?"

"Really an agglomeration of accidental irregularities on the earth's crust are considered beautiful only by those whose sense of proportion has been vitiated. The sea, the wide open plain, the desert, the expanse of sky—these *are* beautiful because immense, and should please rather than winding irregular valleys and rugged rocks."

"And men and women? Do you not allow that they differ in beauty?"

"Not at all; every being, as everything create is neither beautiful nor ugly of itself, each one may be considered as both according to the perception of the observer. The giant toad may consider some other toad to possess the very best shape of anything create. Always amid different surroundings from those to which you have been accustomed even *you* might think the natural contour of the Hottentot Venus more beautiful than the lines of the latest Paris fashions."

"But I do not consider the Paris fashions beautiful."

"That is begging the question," she said severely as the bell brought to a close a discussion to which the learned disquisition of the foreign professor came as a positive relief.

A very few sentences from Mavis Weyland convinced Sterry that she was a woman not of ideas but of disposition.

"The Limitations of Destiny" she did not even pretend to discuss, but in the ten minutes allotted she made Sterry feel that he was a free agent able to reach beyond the deepest dreams of fantasy. She imbued him with a new sense of his importance, of his might; even suggested his duty to himself by expressing to the utmost whatever was within him. He rose Napoleonic, full of grand ideas of his own, and possessed of a high opinion of the sterling good sense of the young girl who had flattered him.

Before he left he had some talk with Iltyd Jones, a mercurial young Welshman, dreamy of eye and bald of head, who had discovered a means of toughening earthenware. Every one had tried to convince him that toughened china was the very last thing any right-thinking person would purchase; that he had wasted his time with the invention, and would waste his energy in proceeding further with the matter. Only Mavis Weyland thought the thing great, he said, and at that the men smiled.

CHAPTER V.

THE FIRST MOVE FORWARD.

THE next day was one of disaster. The Duke of Hallamshire was one of the urbane people who sit enthroned upon the mountain of conventionality and are so unswervingly good-natured that none of the most wronged finds the heart to displace. He expressed himself as deeply interested in the details of the discovery Sterry described, but of its practical value he was not convinced. There was no popular demand for any radical change in the telegraphic service, and unless people clamoured loudly for increased facilities it was much better to allow matters to go on satisfactorily as at present. It was just possible it might be advantageous economically to the Department, and as to that experts would advise when the things had been patented and they had full details and time to study them; but even if economical there, it was very doubtful whether such an advantage would compensate for the very serious dislocation of industries which would necessarily follow if wires were superseded. He advised Sterry to patent the invention; possible he could make it known through the Royal Institution; if not, the engineers of Great George Street might be induced to listen to him.

"In what way would that benefit me?"

The Duke of Hallamshire laughed; it seemed ridiculous that a rich man should expect any benefit from a thing so trivial as an invention. Of course money was no object. Then it was a title Sterry was expecting, and his genial manner congealed to the excessively polite zero of official demeanour.

"The Academies may confer degrees."

"Pah! I can buy as many as I want."

"If you have everything, we can give nothing; we can but thank you as we thank other inventors for largesse in conferring a boon on humanity."

"You have the impudence to thank the men whom you rob?"

"Rob? They give us of their best and are pleased if we accept. We can do very well without new inventions."

Sterry thought the way of the inventor hard to travel.

He went on to Lady Ancaster's, expecting to have a better chance of convincing the Honourable Benjamin B. Fitzroy now that he had interviewed the Duke of Hallamshire.

That sprig of nobility soon undeceived him.

"You have been behind my back with the business, now I must keep my back turned upon it," he said surlily.

Sterry did not mend his humour by answering tartly that it was always "above his head."

Then Warren found him, and in great dudgeon upbraided him for having spoiled all his chances by his too early departure from Lady Kyrwick's.

"What could it matter to any when I went?"

"But you went before the Prince," he repeated, as though it were an unpardonable offence.

"How did I know what time he intended to leave? And why should I stay there all night because a man with whom I have never spoken had a mind to waste his time that way?"

"Etiquette forbade."

"Ah, I'm too old to waste my time in learning useless customs. I have done with Society, Warren."

The courtier tried to explain; but the American was intractable. He meant to be independent again.

It was put down to temper, and Society was ready enough to forgive him if he would amend, for Society was not above recognising the Sterry gold, though it was not to be coerced into recognising the man Sterry as a person of genius. That would be tantamount to conferring a title to aristocracy taking precedence of their lineage in the popular estimation; and if an aristocrat be not popular nowadays, of what use is he to himself or his class?"

The Hon. Benjamin Blanchard Fitzjoy was disappointed; he had schemed to get some of the Sterry millions into the Fitzjoy family, and probably with a less onerous proviso than attached to their last alliance of birth with wealth. The old Jew, Benjamin Moses, had coupled his "gift" with an obligation upon each of his heirs in tail to take his "Christian" name, which was his way of effectually rubbing in the Hebrew taint generation after generation. If Irene Fitzjoy could have been induced to take the American millionaire in training, instead of leaving him to that ass Warren, all might have been well; and now Sterry had looked into Society and withdrawn disgusted, ranging at large, a man with money and ideas. After all, Fitzjoy did not doubt conventionality would be more than a match for him and his dollars, but he would need watching.

Then for a few days Sterry wandered about in a state of great unrest. Alan Winship, who was of a practical turn of mind, suggested that the Sterrygraph should be made use of to found an International News Agency. The invention itself did not strike him as at all out of the way. He induced Iltyd Jones to state what he had done and to give specimens of the new metal—"clear as crystal, strong as steel." Then one day he brought in old Peter Robertson, who for more than a score of years had been saving money in order to patent the "new motor" all the world over; even Boyd Robson gave a few hints he knew of destroying fortresses and sinking ships. Inventions were plentiful as blackberries.

"It is this way," said Alan Winship, between the puffs of his cigarette: "the Robertson motor is no good because old Peter hasn't the money to work it, and never will have. You have money, and so hold the stick at both ends. Take my advice: start an International News Agency, and you will have a powerful lever for other things. It will cost you next to nothing to transmit the news, so you can supply a better service for half the money, and make a good profit. You can make the machines in Spitzbergen or where you please; none but your own agents will know how to use them, so the secret will remain yours."

"That seems easy enough."

"It is—if you have the money. Little Jones wants only money to get the right earth and plenty of sea-water in a place where no factory agent nor industrial spy is likely to pay surprise visits; then he could put that toughened earthenware on the market at a tenth the price of Coalport."

"He can come with me, then."

"What is the matter with you, Bob? You look ferocious," said Willie wonderingly.

"That is the way I feel. It is a shame people cannot get a chance. I am determined to make a way for myself."

"What are you going to do?"

"I do not know."

"Come down to the House of Commons with me to-night and hear a debate. Staley, the member for Hillborough, is to tilt against the Navy Estimates. An armed cruiser built on the Tyne for the Venezuelans has proved on her trial trip superior to anything turned out of the Royal Dockyards; the Venezuelans cannot complete the purchase, and Staley wants the Admiralty to buy her."

"I do not see how that can interest you, Winship."

THE FIRST MOVE FORWARD. 35

"Oh, doesn't it? First, as a matter of policy—we ought to buy her. Of course we sha'n't. We haven't enough common-sense. Second, because I gave the information to Staley, and I want to hear whether he gets an advertisement of " The Industrial Weekly" into the debate, as he ought to do by way of compensation to me for my trouble. Won't you come?"

"No, thanks. Where are the letters, Willie?"

Redhead pointed to a large wicker hamper.

"They have not been coming in so fast lately."

"Not quite, but it is still troublesome to find my own among them. Your aristocratic acquaintance seem to be neglecting you."

"Ah! You have noticed that! I have done with them. They are only like the dead wood on a walnut-tree; they bear no fruit, though they make a good show of timber at other seasons."

"The best fruit is on the highest branches, Bob."

"And to get there some of the dead wood must be knocked off—it will be all the better for the tree."

"To get up the butt to the first fork is the hardest climb. Have you thought how it is to be done?"

"Most people try to just shin up. Some get up by means of a golden ladder; the longer the ladder the easier the ascent, unless they rest it upon dead wood. I am going to get up with a pair of climbing-irons, Willie."

"What *do* you mean?"

"You will see. Now I'm going through the letters."

He lifted as many as he could take in hands and arms on to the table, turned the others out on to the floor, and put the empty basket close to his chair. For a time he worked in silence, opening envelope after envelope, and just glancing at the signature, throwing both as waste into the hamper.

"That Hilda Kewney is the most voluble person I ever met," said Willie.

"Lively enough, isn't she?" remarked Robert, scarcely noticing the interruption.

"If there be many as talkative as she, the Sterrygraph will come as a boon."

"Better present her with a transmitter, then."

"What are you looking for?"

"A letter, of course."

"Oh."

Another armful of letters was lifted from the heap on to the table, and still more hastily scanned and thrown aside.

"Would you mind passing me that book if it is not of use to you as a letter-weight?"

Sterry passed the book in silence, then continued his task. He worked on savagely; it was nearly midnight when he collected the few last stragglers about the floor and put them on the table; a halfdozen open sheets lay there, but the basket was filled high with the cast aside.

"Willie looked up from his book. You haven't found the one you want?"

"No."

"All that came are there. That Miss Kewney wishes you to go with her to-morrow to call on a Miss—Weyland, I think she said."

"Why could you not tell me that before? It would have saved me this labour." And he swept the remaining letters unopened into the basket.

"I did not know."

"At what time? Where?"

"I told her I did not think you would be able to go. If you could, you were to meet at the Woman's Rights Association office."

"That's all right, then."

"Miss Kewney was very entertaining. I say, Bob, I rather like——"

"Eh?"

"The Isocrats."

"Oh yes."

"It is quite refreshing to find some people who know life is a tragedy, and who do not play comedy always."

"Most people act as though it were a pantomime."

"I am going to join the 'isocracy.'"

"Very well; only——"

"What?"

"We may not always reside here, you know."

"That is just what I was going to say. Can we not get a house more conveniently central—a house which would do for the meetings?"

"That is not what I meant. We want no ties, you and I—nothing which will keep us from pursuing our experiments."

"Of course not. But as long as we remain here?"

"I shall not stay long in London."

"By-the-bye, what was the letter for which you were looking?"

"One that has never been written, I expect."

"By Miss Kewney?"

"Wrong."

"Miss Weyland, then?"

"Had you not best go through the list of the Isocrats? Do not bother about it now." Then seeing the perplexed look upon his friend's face, his manner softened, and he added quickly: "We shall not fall out over that, Willie."

"No, no. But when will you go ahead with the Sterrygraph?" he asked, anxious to change the topic.

"By to-morrow night you will be advising me to hold back."

"What do you mean? What are you going to do?"

"Something which may astound you. Good night."

The next morning Robert Sterry, for once in his life, evinced a keen interest in the daily papers. He left early, and was away all day. Miss Kewney waited late at the office, then went round to Fulham, but there was no news of him, and she soon left, evidently disappointed.

Willie Redhead could not understand it: never before had he been ignored by his friend, and it was clear Robert meditated some serious step, and had not asked his advice. For the time the invention lost its interest; his book he neglected, and sat idly drumming on the table with his fingers, gazing vacantly before him.

It was nearly midnight when Robert entered.

"There, I have bought the 'Cuyuni'! What do you think of me?"

"The warship?"

"No other. Nominally I have taken her up for the Venezuelans, but it is understood they will never redeem her. I mean to clear out of this country at the soonest. The guarantee engineers are on board, and I have arranged for a crew to be signed on for six months. You will come, of course!"

"Where are you going?"

"To find a place in Venezuela or somewhere else where we can work in peace and exploit our inventions. Boyd Robson is coming out, so that no time may be lost in getting to work when we decide upon a suitable pitch; and his cousin, a Mr. Kell, happens to be the guarantee engineer the builders have put on board, so we shall have some sort of control over the ship. The Spanish-Americans and Spaniards I shall unship at the first opportunity."

"I do not understand it all. Why did you not tell me?"

"I told you I was going to buy climbing-irons. This pattern pleases me best."

CHAPTER VI.

CONCESSIONS.

THE paragraphs concerning a millionaire's freak had scarcely been the round of the papers when a rumour was published that the " Cuyuni " had been wrecked on the coast of Morocco. A few days later Sterry was in London, but his movements baffled the reporters; the most enterprising of them could discover only that he had purchased or hired a powerful North Sea steam tug, and sent her with an expert diver and a lot of salvage gear to Saffi.

The story Sterry told Redhead was businesslike. On the south coast of Morocco, in the Sus country, they had found a creek in a desolate district which would suit Jones's purpose and his own. The two of them, with an artful Moor, by name Lukeeli, had journeyed inland to Fez, bribed and cajoled a Court favourite, and obtained from the young Shereef leave to establish factories on the river for the manufacture of such transparent steel wares as they presented to him. In exchange he was to have the " Cuyuni." She would keep the Riff tribes in awe, and Sterry undertook to train a crew within twelve months, during which time she was to remain near the conceded territory for the protection of their works, and be wholly under his command. A like vessel had been ordered to take her place when she was finally made over to the Moors.

" We have absolute control of twenty-five miles of coast from the south bank of the stream in front of Fort Chanak, southward towards the Sus, and as much back land as we can occupy, all rent and tax free for ever and no restrictions, except that the erection of places of worship other than mosques is prohibited, and no trade allowed with the natives in arms, explosives, or alcohol. I consider it cheap at a million dollars, which is about what it has cost."

"And the next thing?" asked Willie excitedly.

"Is to plant the right people there. We have planned out how best to utilise the river banks: the secret factories and loading-quays on the north; graving-docks, trading-quays, and repairing-sheds on the south side. Robson is on his way there now with four hundred British navvies to make a start; we have two steamers loading the plant, and schooners with timber are already on the way to Port Cristal —for so we named the river—from Gefle, Kotka, and Miramichi. We have to be smart to get all done before the hot weather begins."

"Who is to help you at the head of the concern?"

"You, of course; then our friends, and their friends, and their friends' friends. Cristallia is to be as clannish as the engine-room of an Atlantic liner."

"But we shall want thousands of workers."

"And we shall get them all, on the rolling snowball plan. Suppose we begin with the Isocrats—a dozen of them. First there is Robson—he is altogether with us, and so are his people; his cousin, Kell, will have charge of the motor factory, for I am going to buy the Robertson motor, out and out, for the good of the concern. Then Winship has promised to get a dozen trustworthy men at once to start the news agency. I can find three dozen mechanics from the old shop at Hartford who will make the instruments; and each will bring in three dozen more as soon as room can be found for them. Then Toller——"

"What! Harry Toller, the accountant? He is quite an ordinary man."

"Just a man of figures; a man of business, but not at all an ordinary man. The first man taken out of the street would not be the equal of Toller, and you know it. He seems ordinary because, as Beatrice Tyacke first pointed out to me, he possesses the genius of common-sense. As soon as I recognised that, I did not see how the republic could be run without Toller."

"Then it is to be a commonwealth?"

"On what other lines could it succeed? We take the Isocratic platform—advancing the welfare of the mass by attending to the wants of the individual; the inventors, the real creators of wealth, our only aristocrats."

Later, after long consultations with Toller and Willie Redhead, he explained his scheme in detail to the Isocrats. When in a few words Toller showed that the plan was feasible their enthusiasm was great. In a neat speech their spokesman, a plain Mr. Smith, thanked the inventor for the chance he had given them of demonstrating the practicability of their theories of government; the colony in Africa would grow into an ideal republic worthy the emulation of every civilised community. They must beware of parasitical growths, guard jealously their own rights, remembering that every modern government was at heart a freebooter. They made the venture under the best possible conditions, carrying war into no one's camp, working unknown industries and exploring fresh fields; their firm belief in the truth that the good of all was only to be obtained through the welfare of each individual would save them from the fate of like enterprises undertaken by men imbued with the altruistic principles which end with national suicide.

Beatrice Tyacke was anxious to know whether the new community would be "white," illuminating and cleansing "that dark Africa Europe has made so red."

Reassured on this point; Madeline Winship asked from what people the colonists would be taken.

There Sterry spoke decisively.

"From among the citizens of the United States and the middle class of Great Britain."

Asked to define the middle class, he held it to range from the master workman to the man who had refused a baronetcy—both inclusive. Personally, he "would give preference to the hardy workers in iron from the North-East Coast and the Midlands—people whose forefathers from generation to generation had breathed iron dust, people inured to drudgery from childhood, and by nature as pugnacious as gamecocks."

Then it was decided that a week should be allowed in which to apply for service with the adventurers; the young members quickly volunteered for employment in Cristallia, the middle-aged and old were content to work for the cause in their native land. Only one Isocrat neglected to apply; Mavis Weyland made no communication whatever. This annoyed Robert Sterry; the reason for it he determined to ascertain. Mavis Weyland was only a pupil teacher in a Kensington Board School, but more might be learned from studying why she refrained than was to be gained from the adherence of the enthusiastic. He obtained her address, and one sultry afternoon set forth in a hansom to call upon her.

He passed quickly through the well-paved streets of the West End, and on and on towards the confines of the great city until he reached a dingy suburb where respectability merges in squalor. A locality teeming with small villas, tenement houses, and sooty terraces; a corner of Kensington wedged in between a great infirmary and the boundaries of a jail, a district in the grip of the speculative builder and incompetent vestryman. The ill-made streets served both as playgrounds for a multitude of children and rubbish heaps for miscellaneous offal; and withal under the too heavy shower from a bulky water-cart, asserted their own true nature of swamp on Thames clay. Dead pigeons were piled high on hampers on a passing cart, black smuts fell thickly from the many chimneys, a hundred stale odours of decay arose from the moistened dust and filth, and the whole life of the place seemed almost to revert to that lower bacillic organism from which, in the golden age, it had arisen.

At the entrance to a long cul-de-sac, blocked by a milk-cart and a coster's shallow, the hansom stopped. Robert alighted and looked up at the neighbouring school buildings—dirty, decaying, and desolate; ugly as a public office, but rising monstrous, in ogre-like importance, from the dreary monotony of puny villas. The cabman might wait where he liked; Robert walked along the court seeking the house he wanted, and stumbled over a child in the gutter in his anxiety to see the number on a door. The terrace was very long, and all the houses were exactly alike; windows and doors both were flung wide open in most, in hope of coaxing the muggy air of the street to mingle with the still more foul air of the little rooms. Two miserably dressed but happy-faced schoolgirls tripped out of one gate, and at the door stood Mavis Weyland, her dress hidden by a long peignoir—dark blue with small white spots, Sterry afterwards remembered—and a common school pencil in her hand.

She drew back into the dusk of the hall as he mounted the steps, and kept her left hand upon the edge of the door as though intending to shut it.

"Ah, Miss Weyland, we have received no application from you to join the industrial community of Cristallia," he commenced lightly.

"No—no, I have not applied."

"Then I should like a talk with you, if I may."

"Will you come in, then, Mr. Sterry?" She backed before him along the little hall, threw open the door into a small sitting-room looking out on the street, and followed him closely.

On the centre table were school books and slates, a vase of drooping flowers; while the end nearest the door was spread with soiled damask cloth and tea-tray. A small metal pot peeped from under a cosy of crazywork, a half-loaf lay prone in a scalloped bread basket, five long red and two round white radishes were limp upon a small blue plate, and a number of buzzing flies dodged about the tiny sugar-basin and the little yellow pat of margarine in its glass dish.

"You will please excuse the disorder," she said quietly; "my girls have only just gone."

"Very rude of me to intrude; you must forgive me." He was seeking a place to put his hat, and noticed on the crowded cheffonier a little heap of hairpins lying on an exercise book, and he looked at her. She blushed, shook the pins down behind the books, and taking his hat from his hand, put it on the cleared surface; and turning, revealed her three long plaits of yellow hair, all kinked by their close coiling, now dangling about her waist.

"The weather is almost unbearable; to-day the schoolroom was like an oven."

"Intolerable; but it is oppressive and stuffy indoors and out. Do not let me keep you from your tea."

"I do not seem to want it now. May I offer you a cup?"

"Thank you, if you take one too."

"I am afraid you will not enjoy it." As she took a second cup and saucer from the cupboard of the cheffonier she went on to explain that the milk they had went sour, and they had long to wait for the coming of the milkman.

"Now, in Cristallia it is always dry, and therefore the heat is nothing; there this heat would not seem oppressive."

"It is the thunder," she interrupted.

"You would like even that better in Cristallia than here."

"If I could go. But I am not free like the others, Mr. Sterry, and I am not yet of age."

"But you are an orphan?"

"I have a guardian, and he would never consent."

"Have you asked him?"

"I know his objections to all 'wild-cat' schemes."

"Then let me ask him? I will undertake to gain his consent."

"It is very good of you, but I must refuse. My uncle made sacrifices in order to place me here; in two or three years, when I have passed all my examinations, I shall be able to maintain myself, and perhaps repay him."

"And it is for that you keep a night school?"

"I do not keep any night school," she said, laughing.

"Then these things——"

"Belong to some of the poorest of our scholars. Some who have neither time nor place in which to prepare their home lessons come in here."

"That is good of you—there is no obligation on your part to trouble with them?"

"That depends on what is meant by obligation; we have to get the children past the Standard—if we can. I found that some had practically no home, others no time; they had babies to mind, errands to run, housework to do, and home lessons were impossible; it was better they should come here for an hour than be out for the cane every day for no fault of their own."

"You must be a favourite with them all."

"I do not know; I used to think so. When I first came here my class tried very hard to please me. Some girls brought me flowers, others fruit, one brought an egg, I remember; yes, and one even bought me a cane. Then I found a poor little mite in tears because she had nothing to give me—no pence, no friends, and no sort of a home—so I stopped all presents. Perhaps they were only given with a view to getting into my good favour or from fear of what I might do to them, poor little things! However, they do not seem to love me the more that I have tried to be just."

"Yet you like the work?"

"Not so much as I expected I should; it is all so different from what I thought it would be. Inside it is so noisy, and close, and stuffy, and Miss Malcolm is not my ideal mistress; her cane is going all day and every day. No wonder there are scenes. I had a near escape to-day!"

"From what?"

"The usual thing. One of the girls had been punished, and her mother and friends armed themselves and came to avenge the assault. They hid in a public-house until school was over; then this savage, half intoxicated woman ran at me like a mad thing, for I chanced to be first. She was just about to claw my face, when the mother of some other girl came between us and said: 'Not that 'un, 'Ria! her's a hangel, 'er is!' and that gave time for the others to get back into school until the police came. I hope they won't have me for a witness, but I expect they will."

"Leave it all, and come with us!"

"How I should like to! But you know I cannot."

"All the others are going."

"I shall miss Madeline Winship, and Beatrice, and some of the others very much. It was so nice to listen to their schemes for making the world better and life more wholesome. I always came away from the meetings feeling stronger and happier; it is because I believe them to be right that I am convinced I must not shirk my duty here."

"You mistake. They teach that every one should so live as to get the most from life, the greatest well-being for self, and thus the greatest good for all."

"If I left I should despise myself."

"But, Miss Weyland, even from your own point of

view, your duty is to come with us. We want you. You can do more for our good, more for the general good, by helping as we want you to, than you ever will here at work others can do."

"No, no. I have thought it all out; I must not go."

The hansom came into the court; the noiseless wheels, the jingling bells on the horse's neck, attracted attention; and when the driver turned his cab, then pulled up by the kerb right opposite the open window at which Robert was sitting the dwellers in the court became interested.

"Miss Weyland, you may leave all this. It is my misfortune to have had left me more money than I know how to spend wisely for the common welfare. You can help me do good with this money. I ask you, I beg of you, not to refuse."

There was an earnestness in his manner that alarmed her. She rose from her chair and stood against the chimney-piece, with its dusty mirror, facing him.

"And then, if you really do not like this African scheme, we have not gone so far yet we cannot draw back. I thought it the best way to—to advance humanity, but there may be others as good. It shall be as you wish, if only you will share fortune with me."

She understood him then, and stood for a minute irresolute. A little knot of loungers were just outside admiring the horse and listening to the driver's account of his journey to Epsom the week before. She and he heard each word distinctly.

She shook her head, then raised her eyes to his and looked at him steadily.

"You must not draw back—for me, or for any one."

"With you Cristallia will be a success; unless you join us, I cannot promise that we shall make any headway."

"You will succeed, do not fear; you and the others will succeed. I shall often think of you all; when you have forgotten me, for you will have no time to think of aught but your work in Cristallia—at least, I hope not, for it must grow into an empire some day soon. I should only hinder there; here, I am of some use."

He saw that she was resolute; he could not reason with her; but he was loth to leave.

"I shall start the day after to-morrow for Port Cristal; there is plenty of time to think over what I have said, and, I hope, time for you to decide as I wish you to. Now, before I go, tell me, is there nothing I can say to convince you? Is there nothing, then, I can do to help you before I go?"

"You are so clever—if you do not mind, for a minute—will you please look at this, and tell me how it is done?"

She handed him an examination paper, and took up the open exercise book with which she had been engaged previous to his arrival.

"It is that question about the tank, with two taps, A and B, to fill it, and the tap C emptying it; you see, something like it is put at every examination, and if I cannot work it out I shall not pass. Edith Stokes failed through that very thing this time, and she does not understand it yet."

Sterry signed for her to sit down, took the pencil in his hand, then commenced good-humouredly to explain. He stated the various items with a swift, firm stroke until a plait of yellow hair fell light as a skein of silk upon the back of his hand and stopped it suddenly. With a hasty movement she threw the long tress back, and gathering the plaits together, tucked them under the opposite arm.

"I really must apologise. I—my head ached so badly this afternoon that—yes, it is seven-eighths, not five."

Sterry was working again.

"Then it is mis-stated: you see why? If the tank is seven-eighths full to begin with, before the tap A has run thirteen of its allotted twenty-three minutes, an overflow pipe would be useful; the question, therefore, is absurd."

"Do you think it is a 'catch'?" she asked eagerly.

"A 'catch'? I cannot say. Who can fathom the shallowness of intellect possessed by the average school examiner? If this 'catch,' as you call it, be a mean subterfuge to trap the unwary, then the action is too despicable for words and is almost beyond justification by kicks. If it be an oversight, the would-be teachers ought themselves to be sent to the whipping-block. The man is an imbecile anyway, or he would be something better than a school examiner."

"Yes, yes; but what is the rule?"

For half an hour or more he expounded, simplified, worked, suggested, encouraged, explained. The cab horse was becoming restive, the driver impatient, the throng of idlers noisy and free in their talk. He would have continued, but his hand was stayed again; a large hot tear fell upon his wrist and trickled down on to the paper. He worked on to the end in silence.

"There, now, do you think you understand it, Miss Weyland?"

"I think so—thank you—yes." She frowned at the figures, then bit her lip.

He saw that she did not understand, felt that probably she never would understand, and grew angry with the fates that oppressed her. It seemed to him abominable that conventional people should demand such a sacrifice of energy from her in attempting to solve the futile conundrums of their stupidly clever officials when she was ready to yield all that was best and most enduring in human nature.

"Miss Weyland! Won't you listen to me? Can't you see that all this drudgery is killing you? What is the good of it all? Don't you feel that it is to no purpose? That to succeed is useless? Life has a more serious purpose than the painful acquisition of empty knowledge of that sort. Come! In Cristallia there will be a school where you may teach people how to live wisely. Come, let me take you away now! Come!"

"I dare not!—I dare not! Please do not ask me!"

"You shall not wreck your own life—and mine. You shall come, Mavis!"

He moved towards her, and she retreated before him hastily. Nearing the door she looked at him so pleadingly that for a moment he hesitated. She saw that he loved her, and knew then that she had only herself to dread. For an instant her ideal obscured him, and then she spoke, falteringly, and shaking like an aspen-leaf, but with a tone that carried conviction to Sterry.

"I can help you only by staying here."

"But——"

"No, no; please do not. Good-bye, Mr. Sterry, good-bye!"

She followed him to the door, then closed it and sat down as far from the window as she could and buried her face in her hands. She heard his tread on the steps; noticed that he paused a moment on the footpath hesitating; then he called loudly to the driver: "Métropole," and the horse started forward. The throng of idlers hurried to the entrance of the court "to see him go" down the road, but she was motionless, and knew no more until her landlady was standing over her with a tumbler of water in her hand and suggesting the advisability of going at once to bed.

She stumbled up the dark stairs, and in her room cried herself to sleep, and happily heard nothing of the storm that raged an hour before midnight and made the air of the morning so much fresher and purer than that of yesterday that she went to work blithely, the events of the evening but a distant memory.

Sterry sailed for Port Cristal and stayed there; Alan Winship, Toller, and the rest joined him. The others went to and fro, but Redhead and Sterry were always in Cristallia, and had no easy time. Beatrice Tyacke told Mavis Weyland that progress in the African colony was very slow; the letters she had received told only of flies and mud-holes full of stinking turtles, sandy wastes, great storms, heaps of rubbish and scaffolding.

The women grew anxious, but the men would allow none to enter Cristallia until everything had been prepared, and time after time the day was deferred; then at last the boldest of the lady Isocrats got on board a steamer and went out unauthorised.

CHAPTER VII.

IN CRISTALLIA.

THE Honourable Benjamin B. Fitzjoy prided himself upon his encyclopædic knowledge of modern geography gained at first-hand. While his co-legislators were recuperating with the aid of golf-sticks or shot-guns, he was to be found "'neath alien skies" studying politics in his own fashion in some out-of-the-way spot. In a borrowed steam yacht he sailed for Morocco to ascertain whether or not the North-West African question could be brought within the domain of practical politics at an early date. An astute British Consul hinted that the solution of the problem would possibly be found in the newly established colony on the Sus; so Fitzjoy packed off his friends and the yacht to Grand Canary, and with Britain's representative sailed from Mogador in a trading schooner for Port Cristal.

It was nearing sunset when they arrived off the entrance to the creek; a swift-gliding, noiseless tug came alongside, put a pilot and harbour officer on board, then took the craft in tow, and by a winding channel led them past the outer anchorage, round Cristal point to the inner harbour. Then the country opened out like a fairy scene. Along the north shore a wide quay and boulevard, the white walls of factories, bright cupolas, chimney-stacks like minarets, dome kilns, and long workshops with verandahs and gardens; on the summit the conning tower, the Capitol, and the arsenal. On the south side the low land by the shore was of greater extent; the Guest House on the quay stood in its own large garden; farther up stream were the warehouses, huge stores, and many buildings, white-painted staiths and jib-cranes, and a shipyard as scrupulously clean as the tiled verandah before the harbour-master's home. An English steamer and four Norwegian sailing ships were moored alongside the quay; in the river lay two great armed cruisers and a smaller more graceful craft—half pleasure-yacht, half gunboat. Behind them all, where the ravine narrowed and the banks rose steep, the river was spanned by a suspension bridge, elegant as the threads of a spider's web.

The streets were almost deserted; on the quays a few Moorish sentinels were pacing to and fro; somewhere amid the trees a band was playing, and above all could be heard the steady roar of falling water from some distant torrent. It grew dark, and lights glowed from the houses on the high land, through the glass roofs of the factories, and along the quays; then the warships turned their search-lights on the intruding vessel, keeping her under close scrutiny the night through.

Early the next morning a launch came alongside and brought the visitors to the quay before the Guest House, where Robert Sterry was waiting to receive them. He politely bade them welcome and lodged them with a bland Swiss, but showed no intention of gratifying their curiosity as to the topography of Cristallia.

"Will you tell us how you run the concern?" asked Fitzjoy with the persistence of a journalist.

"It is run on the mutual confidence plan, in the interest of us all. I was taking my turn in the factories last night, or you might have come ashore then. No one else here knew you personally, and unless you are known to some one of us who will guarantee your behaviour you would not be allowed to land. I dare not take you across to the north shore, and for you to enter either of the factories is out of the question. We are bound to guard our secrets since even the most civilised among the civilised nations would not hesitate to rob us of them."

"Everything is fair in—politics."

"We recognise that opinion; therefore keep two guardships—and other things."

"What are two ships? We could send fifty steamers to-morrow if we meant to take you. Cristallia exists solely by the goodwill of the nations."

"And their mutual jealousy. If you decided to take Cristallia by force, others would try to forestall you; there would be a general scramble, and while our assailants were knocking their heads against each other outside, we hope we could escape."

"How do you guard against treachery within?"

"All our people are contented; it is their interest as much as mine to have the secret kept; moreover, all are honourable; and all are convinced that the life here is better than they could lead elsewhere."

"What extraordinary people! Wherever did you find them?"

"In the too crowded cities of England and the United States; in the barren lands of Scandinavia; a few have been attracted from other countries—not many; we have no opening for traders, we want only producers."

"How did you eliminate the trader?"

"We never allowed him a footing. From the first the State has been the only trader; the buyers, the salesmen, the labourers — one and all — are the salaried servants of the Commonwealth, just as are the postmistresses you employ to sell postage-stamps. It was easier to begin than it would be to convert; we had to feed, lodge, and clothe the navvies we brought in to make the harbour and railway, and we have continued as we began."

"Then none can rise in your Commonwealth?"

"Only by inventing something. The inventors are the real creators of wealth; the State collects and pays to them ten per cent. of the sale price obtained for their wares; the State also makes ten per cent. or more profit for itself, levies an import duty of ten per cent. on all goods, and then sells at cost price. An export duty at the same rate on native produce shipped completes the taxation, which provides more than enough to cover all expenses and pay back instalments of the borrowed capital."

"Cristallia must be a dull place for the ambitious."

"Hardly, or exile could not be the most dreadful punishment. Our chief difficulty is in getting our people away for even a short holiday. A free passage out and home is insufficient inducement."

"How do you govern?"

"By the voice of the people. We thought of adopting the Indian Penal Code intact, but so far have no use for it. Some of the labourers have been troublesome, but they could always be shipped back to their native land. Only the factory hands could possibly harm us, and we have them pretty tight. One blustering fellow who thought he had learned something, threatened to divulge the secret when he got home, but the two men who had guaranteed his fidelity showed him what the result would be to them, and he is now as much ours as any of the rest. If the three had gone, they must have left four of the best friends of two of them to stand the brunt of their misconduct; in the unlikely event of the seven conspiring, at least eight—the guarantors of the four—would have been at the mercy of we others; that is the way we hold the manufacturing secrets so close. A fellow who misbehaved out of the factory was 'sent to Coventry' until he apologised and made what restitution he could. He was penitent within a week. Another, who in a passion attacked a fellow worker for some clumsiness, was threatened with banishment if found outside the factory during the next month. He was hidden within doors, and had to depend upon his mates for food and other conveniences; they soon became sorry for him, and their sympathy made the bonds closer than they were before. Another scamp, who savagely attacked his wife, had similar treatment, and was obliged to cater for himself. Of course his wife was soon beseeching all to get him liberated; but he had been ordered the penalty by a jury of twelve of his mates and neighbours, seven of whom had to guarantee his future good behaviour before he was reinstated, and the trouble he had to convince them of his intentions quite cured him. By leaving the jury to fix the penalty there is a tendency to too great severity, but by making a pardon conditional upon the jury personally guaranteeing future conduct you bring about a reformation in character."

"What do you do with the confirmed criminals, the incorrigibly vicious?"

"We have none."

"What is the secret?"

"Madeline Winship would tell you that it is all a question of diet: 'if you underfeed, you get crime; if you overfeed, you beget vice.' That's the formula, isn't it, Madeline?" and he turned to his companion, who nodded acquiescence. "I should say it is because we get rid of the undesirable—ship them off at once."

"Then the stories about the oubliette, life-long imprisonment, death by torture, and mysterious disappearances are all wild inventions?"

"Probably based on the lethal chamber Willie Redhead built near the capitol, so that any tired of life could find a pleasurable way out. It is the

IN CRISTALLIA.

only luxurious apartment in Cristallia, and every evening when the concert begins in the public gardens it is filled with a poisonous gas from the Iltydium factory. There have been no suicides yet."

"Quite an ideal colony. And the natives?"

"Are as free as the rest. We have no forced labour, no slaves, no black men in wire cages, as is the custom in a British colony."

"I have nothing to do with the Colonial Office."

"Nor I with Britain."

"But you are one of Her Majesty's subjects?"

"I think not. My father did not take out his papers of naturalisation until long after I was born; but at any time I can become a citizen of the United States of America if I cease to be a commoner of the Industrial Community of Cristallia."

"But Cristallia is not recognised as an independent state."

"Not by Britain, as yet. The Storthing has already acknowledged us; the day after to-morrow His Majesty the King of Sweden and Norway will be represented in Cristallia by a resident Consul— a Mr. Ulitsen, who has acted both in the United States and in a British Colony. Your man will come later; the Norwegian will be the doyen of the diplomatic corps here.

The Under Secretary and the Vice-Consul exchanged glances.

"We cannot recognise your independence, but if you want our protection you can have it on terms."

"Only by forfeiting some liberty; to that our people would never consent."

"But you can. Confound it, we don't want Morocco to become a second Turkey and an everlasting question; and though I say it unofficially, it is nevertheless true, Britain will not allow any new independent State being founded in Africa; there are far too many already, and if you want to attempt empire-making you must try somewhere else."

"That is candid; but I am too good a Republican ever to attempt empire-making."

"Africa is no place for republics. African republics are a standing menace to British paramountcy. South America is the place for you Cristal makers; go somewhere near Cosmé and rival the 'Freebrotherhoods,' and work in peace."

"We are here, and here we shall remain. We harm none; do not interfere with their markets, their industries, or their politics. If you do not like us, remove us if you can. What do you say, Madeline?"

"It would not be right," remarked the girl simply.

The Honourable Benjamin put up his monocle and looked at the speaker in his sternest forensic manner.

"My good lady, don't you know that whatever the majority wishes is right, and whatever it disapproves is wrong?"

"No, unfortunately—or the world would not be so wicked as it is."

"What an antiquated philosophy! I cannot argue from such a premiss. Must it be ultima ratio regum? *That* you will understand."

"You know that would be wrong!" retorted the girl angrily.

"Really? You forget that in modern policy expediency has taken the place once said to have been occupied by morals. How else could one tell right from wrong?"

"That is right which you may tell openly to all without apology to any; all else is wrong—and you know it."

"Hardly practical. Your manufacturing secrets, then, are diabolically wicked since they may be spoken of to none." And he chuckled.

Madeline pressed her lips.

"It is not that we should blush to speak, but it would shame the honest to hear; therefore we forbear until you can guarantee that the producer shall not be robbed of his wage."

"We must go our own way; in time it will be the turn of Cristallia—for we are civilising Africa by degrees."

"As Pizarro civilised Peru," said the girl scornfully. And she walked away.

"You will find Cristallia hard to overcome, Fitzjoy—in time we may have friends to help us; why don't you bring England into line?"

"It is the queerest fad of all time. It won't succeed; but if it should, Cristallia will be a standing menace to Europe and to the civilised world. I should say it would die out very soon from inherent dulness."

"You talk with Iltyd Jones as to its dulness. Man, do you not think working new inventions, discovering fresh forces in nature, developing novel processes, the opposite of dull? We travel; but not in a known groove; we get fresh experiences every day—even new diseases plague us. Dull indeed! Do you find it dull trying to convert Radicals?"

"Never try; it is too foolish—and futile as the labours of Sisyphus. Good Tories are born, not made."

"Cristallians too! Our ethics are on a different plane from those of the average politician. We shall never understand each other, Mr. Secretary."

"Oh yes, we shall; later on, Mr. President."

"I am not even the President. Willie Redhead is the chief commoner in Cristallia."

"But you are chancellor of the exchequer and real ruler. You can make Cristallia British territory if you like. If you do not, some one else may."

"You could ruin us easily; but you would not care to take the only way there is to do it."

"And that is——?"

"Giving the British the rights and privileges our people have."

"I think our people would prefer British independence to such liberty as you enjoy in Cristallia. Why, where are your women? I have scarce seen a skirt since I landed."

"They are in their proper place."

"A harem?"

"No; the very top of the State. Women and men have equal rights and privileges in Cristallia, but practically the lady Isocrats govern the place. Half a dozen of them rushed out here more than a year ago and put things to rights. We meant to have all things ready for them, but they determined that the houses in which they would have to live should be built just as they wanted them; and they are. You see that great half-finished building yonder?"

"The ruin?"

"It is as far as we ever got with a great schoolhouse. The ladies stopped that. They have a notion for education in the home, or at any rate in classes, not a barrack. They keep the whole community close-knit, solid, and progressive. They rule by love, and not a complaint is ever heard against them."

"H'm! Love is but the spirit of sex incarnate—and a mischievous devil too. There will be lively times in Cristallia by-and-bye."

"We shall be able to manage our own affairs, if other nations do not interfere. We are here because we believe a higher civilisation than any current in Europe is possible; I do not think we shall fail in doing so little as that, but we hope to get very far ahead, and in a short time. It is for that we set such store upon our secret inventions; they bring us wealth with a minimum expenditure of labour—six hours is now the average, in five years' time we shall reduce it to three, and the rest of the time not necessary to recreation we are striving after higher things. Our experimental workshops and laboratories are always full of ardent inventors. In fact, we are all like the Black Country locksmith who when he knocked off work did a bit of forging on the anvil. Something will come of it all; but of this you may be sure, we shall guard our secrets, and even if we are turned out of Africa by force we shall recommence elsewhere at once."

"And how about that railway of yours to the Atlas?" asked the Vice Consul.

But Robert would say no more.

The schooner lay in the harbour three days, and Fitzjoy and his companion could sometimes be seen walking or riding about the south town. The first Consul came, and there was a banquet and holiday in his honour. Fitzjoy was ignored, and at the conclusion of the festivities put out to sea.

He had not been gone many hours when Baillé, the keeper of the Guest House, sent a letter he had found up to the Capitol. It was from John A. Snyder, a foreman in the Robertson motor factory, and pleaded for an interview with Fitzjoy, to whom, presumably, it had been addressed.

They sent for Snyder, but he could not be found. It appeared that he had applied for leave to go into the "interior," and this had been granted; but as to where he had gone, or why, none could tell.

CHAPTER VIII.

A RENEGADE.

WILLIE REDHEAD was one evening sitting in his room watching some experiments with a new form of transmitter, when Beatrice Tyacke, who was in charge of the instrument room, came in, pale as a ghost, to say that Toller had just sent word that Snyder was in London trying to negotiate the sale of the Robertson motor, and he wanted instructions.

"Shoot him at sight! Stay a minute; where's Sterry? Send for him at once. Then summon the Council. Tell Toller to keep us well informed."

They had to wait for Boyd Robson to get back from El-Aksa, and by that time they learned from Lukeeli that a Moor named Dreis, a harbour boatman, had ferried Snyder and two strangers across the harbour from the Guest House Quay to the north shore, the night of the festival. Morven Kell, who was one of his guarantors, knew little of him; Jake Hanlan, the other, believed he was a German whose real name was Schneider, but he had lived long in America, and whatever he might be, his vacuum valve was as original as anything old Peter Robertson himself had produced. Now he was a renegade all remembered that they had never really liked the man. As to the best thing to be done in present circumstances, most were for taking him, by hook or by crook, alive or dead.

"We must have him!" shouted Willie Redhead. "It is a matter of life and death to the Commonwealth. If any one succeeds in stealing one of our secrets, there will be no rest for us until they have them all."

Winship thought Snyder would be able to do very little with the motor; practically no one knew of it, as its use had been confined to Cristallia, and the dozen or more cargo ships which had been converted to the principle had created little surprise in foreign ports.

Toller soon undeceived them. Snyder was quite determined to exploit the invention, and was merely casting about for the most advantageous offer. Probably he would start a factory in Belgium or Luxemburg; some parasitical State whose neutrality was guaranteed by the Great Powers would most surely ultimately secure it. Snyder himself had gone to Brussels.

"We have hit the Belgian glass industry pretty hard with our Iltydium wares, and they will consider this a fair exchange. Can we fight Belgium? Is it worth while trying?" asked Robson, gnawing at his finger-nails.

"It has not come to that yet. My proposition is that we require Snyder's guarantors—Morven Kell and Jake Hanlan—to bring the renegade before this Council for trial. Let them command whomsoever and whatsoever they will, but bring him here they must and shall!" And Sterry brought his fist down like a sledge-hammer on the Board table.

"Agreed—agreed—agreed!"

"That settles it, then," said Kell quietly; "Sterry himself must accompany us and show how the thing is to be done."

"I am willing. My idea is to take the 'Gleam'; if she is all we think her, then we have the fastest vessel afloat. Snyder is sure to cross the Channel sooner or later. We will hold up the packet and take him."

"And after?" asked Beatrice Tyacke.

"There will be international complications, which we must wriggle out of as best we can. We must show people this sort of robbery cannot be done with impunity; we'll risk our all on it, as we have already done in founding Cristallia."

Two days later the "Gleam" put to sea and headed north. Sterry laid his plans with some care, and moored off Deal before Snyder had returned from the Continent. The little ship lay at anchor in the roads until their agents ashore signalled, two hours before midnight, that Snyder was leaving Ostend by the Dover packet. Then they got under way, took the tampons out of their guns, and went out to meet her.

The night was dark, with some rain, and a fresh breeze from the south-west. Once beyond the three-mile limit, they put out all lights and sped ahead at the rate of thirty miles an hour. It was impossible to mistake the "Princesse Henriette" steaming south at top speed. She had barely passed the "Ville de Douvres" when the "Gleam" bore down upon her. Some passing steamers and sailing ships turned from their course when the fast-racing man-of-war rushed by, but the mail boat, fearing nothing, blew her whistle and was held to her course. Suddenly the searchlight flashed upon her from the conning tower of the "Gleam" and instantly disappeared. This was the first intimation the crew of the packet had that their ship was the object point of the rapidly approaching vessel. She came right for their midships, stem on, but was slowing down. The frightened Belgian had the helm put hard-a-starboard and the engines reversed. The "Princesse Henriette" had turned completely round when the "Gleam," at the same pace, ran right alongside. No sooner did the bulwarks touch the paddle-box than grappling-irons were out, snap-hooks attached to wire cables were fastened to the rigging fore and aft, and the blaze of light that suddenly burst forth on deck revealed the muzzles of two six-inch guns aimed directly at the steamer's hull.

Forty Moors, armed with revolvers and sabres, scrambled after Jake Hanlan and Boyd Robson on to the paddle-box. The captain demanded an explanation, and was referred to Sterry, who shouted at him from the conning tower. While captain, crew, and passengers protested, Robson and the others sought for Snyder. Hanlan found him in the second-class saloon, fast asleep. He was dragged on deck, his luggage pulled out from the heap under the tarpaulin, and as soon as all had been transferred to the "Gleam" the warps were loosed and the vessels parted.

Sterry had no intention of being caught; they raced the "Gleam" back to Port Cristal for all she was worth, and on arrival there found that the "outrage" up to the present had produced nothing worse than newspaper paragraphs and letters from indignant passengers.

CHAPTER IX.

DEFENCES.

THE Isocrats waited until Harry Toller came to Cristallia before they put Snyder upon his trial. The letters the prisoner had upon him fully confirmed his guilt: they did more—their contents could be construed only as an unfriendly act towards the Commonwealth by the Belgian Government. It seemed unlikely that, with such documents in their hands, Belgium would attempt any reprisals.

There was some difference of opinion as to what might be done with Snyder. Redhead, Robson, and Kell were for making short work of him, either by drowning, shooting, or the lethal chamber. Beatrice Tyacke, Madeline Winship, and Hilda Kewney objected on principle; Sterry, Toller, and Alan Winship on grounds of expediency—if the worst came to the worst, something might be gained for Cristallia by surrendering Snyder. It was decided to imprison him in the Capitol until he should invent something of equal value to the community as the invention he had tried to steal.

Asked what he had to say in extenuation of his conduct, he quoted the creed of the Isocrats: " Every man is entitled to live the life he feels he needs to develop what is best in his nature"—"To help others is the highest service one can render to one's self."

"You forget 'Let no man take the life of his brother to feed his own,'" interrupted Beatrice Tyacke.

"That is what you Isocrats are doing; the glass, porcelain, and earthenware industries of France, Belgium and Germany are being ruined by you with your Jonesware and Iltydium."

"And you think to right matters by robbing us of the motor and selling it to Belgium for a million francs? Would you or the makers of steam-engines benefit the more by that transaction?" asked Toller.

Redhead interposed.

"Snyder must stay here until he invents something for us as useful as the motor has proved."

"Then I shall be here all my life!"

"Where you will be able to do less harm than anywhere else."

The Moorish guards took him away to a suite over the lethal hall, and the meeting became even less formal than its wont.

"That is the easiest part of the matter we have to settle. Shall we make the Belgians any offer of compensation?" asked Toller uneasily.

"With the letters in our possession? Let them get compensation if they can," answered Sterry.

"We have no defences."

"And they have no battleships."

"The 'Ville d'Anvers' is ready for sea by this."

"They won't risk sending her here. But our defences are not what they ought to be, Robson. We are not going ahead fast enough."

"H'm! I like that! The defences are right enough; it is the principle that is all wrong."

"What do you mean by that, Boyd?" asked Hilda Kewney, leaning forward anxiously.

"I mean that the defences are no good. No defences are any good. In fisticuffs the best way to defend yourself is to hit the other man in the eye. Now you all understand what I mean."

"But our elaborate precautions—our first-zone, the mid-zone, and the outer-zone? Sha'n't we be quite safe when all the mines are laid and the self-acting guns in position?"

"No, we shall never be safe. They are all right in their way, but they do not make Cristallia impregnable, and it is no use deluding ourselves that they do."

"But the harbour is safe, isn't it, Morven? If not, we will put down more mines," said Sterry.

"I don't know where you'll find room for them; there is hardly a free channel now from beyond the breakwater right up to the quay. I was out in one of the 'crabs' to-day, and we were no sooner off one lot of guncotton than we fouled another."

"We'll make the harbour quite safe. Put two more charges of five hundred pounds, one each side of the channel by the bar. And you, Boyd, start another line of sunk forts to the south of the outer zone."

"We can do both, but neither will save us."

"Then Iltydium will! There's nothing like Iltydium!" And Jones slapped his knee. "I have been making an alloy with tungsten, just enough to make the metal opaque—and a very little tungsten goes a long way in that. There's a lot of gas given off in the process, and it is practically waste. I have got it in tanks, hoping to recover it somehow. You have only to take that gas by a pipe into the sea; as it bubbles up through the water it unites with chloride of sodium and explodes as soon as it reaches the surface. I can make the outer harbour a mass of flame, seething like a cauldron of boiling tar, and keep the fire up for seventy-four hours; that will keep every one off."

"A good idea, but it's no use; they'll shell us to ruins miles beyond the shore. We want men, not machines," said Robson obstinately.

"Men? Then take the two thousand navvies you have on the railway up at El-Aksa," said Sterry.

"What good would they be? After three years' drilling they would not be better than the mercenaries of any other country—not even as good. It is not the quantity I trouble so much about as the quality."

"What is the matter with the quality? Our workers at Cristallia are better on the average than you will find elsewhere." And Sterry seemed annoyed.

"Well, let me enrol the workers in a defence corps. I could trust them better than those beggars on the south side. They are not to be depended upon over there, not one of them. They are all right as men, but not as men for Cristallia. There's Will Perkins, for instance, the best gunner we have. But he would not line a gun against the Union Jack to save his life. And why? Simply because his brother was once a gunner in the 'Collingwood.' And that sentiment goes through the lot. We have men like Speke, Turner, and Adams, who have been retired from the Indian Civil Service, and they're as thoroughly English as the lot of jolly young beggars under them. Though they were spun at Sandhurst or disappointed of a career with the colours in some other way, they still serve 'the widdy' as faithfully as any hero of Kipling's. They're here because they think it is the best thing they can do for themselves; but they would sell Cristallia to-morrow, and count any sedition which would bring us under the British flag honourable."

"We are not cosmopolitan enough yet to be national," said Hilda Kewney decisively.

"That's not the point. We want people here who think and feel as we do about Cristallia: any others are only a danger."

"In what way?"

"Why, in this way: there's a reaction setting in against our strict manner of living. As for our ethics, what do army men care for ethics? They don't want to learn all their lives. They've done with that; they think they know. Now, any sort of church service they might attend, but such lectures and discussions as we have compel them to think. They don't like that. What do they care for the higher life?"

"It is very sad, after all Madeline has done for them," said Beatrice Tyacke.

"You have done your share too, Miss Tyacke, but what are the results?"

"I think I understand it right enough," interrupted Alan Winship. "People will submit to a theocracy, or a monarchy, or a bureaucracy, even a democracy, but they'll never learn to govern themselves. To expect them to be content with a code of ethics and a string of maxims instead of a creed is sheer folly. It's ranking the nature of the average man far too high."

"What is the average man?" asked Toller.

"Why, Snyder," interposed Robson quickly. "There's an average man for you. Any one can see he has been drilled in Prussia, and he could throw any one of us out of the window easily; but he could not do the same with that crafty scamp Lukeeli, who is an average man too; and old Kaid Mahmoud at El-Aksa would settle the pair of them quickly, for as an animal that big Mohammedan is more than average good."

"But really, Mr. Robson, our people are all better morally than those."

"Excuse me, Miss Winship, you are far too forgiving. I know what happened while we were all away on the 'Gleam.' Yes, comrades, there was almost a revolution here in Cristallia. Madeline Winship and Beatrice Tyacke prevailed with the ringleaders to forego any attempt to seize the works; appealed to all that was good in their nature not to shed blood, and obtained the promise they required on condition that the whole matter was to be hushed up. But I know what neither Madeline nor Beatrice yet know: the attempt was to be made the following night, and none who resisted was to be spared. Luckily the 'Gleam' was spied in the offing just in time. The conscience-stricken cowards funked at the last moment; and for a time Cristallia is safe."

"How do you know all this, Boyd?" asked Jones, his face blanching.

"There is always an informer. He told me because he hopes to be rewarded. I knocked him down to begin with. Lukeeli has him in charge just now. Toller will see that he gets home all right."

"Yes, yes, it is quite true. I do not know who is to blame for it," said Jones.

"Is it really true that only the coming of the 'Gleam' prevented them?" asked Madeline, the tears starting to her eyes.

"Undoubtedly that was the sole reason. The wretches!"

"It is ineffably sad," sighed Beatrice Tyacke, hiding her face in her hands, while Madeline sobbed convulsively, and the men looked at each other in wonderment and silence.

At last Alan Winship spoke.

"I'll not believe they're all bad on the south side. There is little Mrs. Speke, as good a woman as ever stood in shoes. Cheer up, Madie!"

"We will find out what the grievance is and meet it," said Toller in his business-like way.

"What they want is license to do what they like —to trade and rob each other and the natives, and make this place like any other colony, and themselves rich."

"O Mr. Robson!" gasped Madeline.

"They have been trying to persuade the factory hands that now they have mastered the secrets they could exploit the things to their own advantage—become millionaires almost, and be honoured in their own country."

"We'll clear the whole lot out," said Sterry angrily.

"Where will you find better men to take their places? They keep order well, know how to manage the Moors and blacks; and but for their confounded old-fashioned notions, we should get on together all right. Better put up with what we have got than take fresh stuff of much the same sort—eh, Toller?"

"They think we fancy ourselves superior to them," interrupted Madeline, "that as inventors we disregard whatever other merits they may have. I have told them again and again that we are all equal, with equal rights and privileges; but they say they have no talent or genius for inventing things, and only inventors can get on here—only inventors in the inner ring—only inventors on the executive. You do not know what jealousy there is."

"And if we give way they will make short work of the community, if they mean to wreck it," said Toller.

"Nothing would please most people better than to see Cristallia go smash," said Hilda Kewney. "I do not know that I should mind so much, as I know we have all done our utmost."

"No, that is not enough, Hilda," said Beatrice Tyacke. "To fail is not only to die in vain, but to make fresh difficulties for reformers who follow us."

"That is true enough. The world is governed by tradition; every law of the civilised is as truly the outcome of custom as the ridiculous etiquette of savages. We must not fail; it will but confirm tradition's cruel rule." Winship looked towards Redhead, who remained stolidly silent through it all.

"Why cannot those who do not agree with us leave us alone?" asked Jones.

"Perhaps, after all, Beatrice, we shall not die quite in vain; no reformer ever does. The upholders of tradition see some little spark of sense in a part of every attempted reform, and, when wise, take more than a fraction of what they see," said Madeline, brightening up a little.

"Aye, a thousandth part of what is the least worth adopting; that is what makes progress so slow," grumbled her brother savagely.

"But perhaps they will not let Cristallia die after all; some will have charity and protect it," said Beatrice Tyacke with some confidence.

"Charity? What good ever came from living on charity?" asked Robson quite angrily. "Was the British Empire fostered by the charity of her enemies —or even of her friends? If we are to do any good to ourselves or to the world, we have got to make others accept our faith, make them adhere to our standard of ethics, live up to our rules of conduct until the practice becomes habitual. They have got to be made to do right until they do it so naturally they think it is intuitional. That's the task we have."

"But how is that to be done, Mr. Robson?"

Robson clenched his fist and put it up before him.

"You see that fist, Miss Tyacke? You can feel this muscle. That is what every task has to be done with, after all. If you look into history, or use your eyes, you will find that the British Empire has been made and is maintained by John Bull's knuckles. With them, and with them alone, England has forced a higher civilisation on the world. It was not Irish fervour, nor Welsh poesy, nor Scottish mysticism that carried Britain to the front in the race of the nations for supremacy. Scotch, Welsh, and Irish went against those hard knuckles of John Bull's until they had more than enough of them. No Celtic glamour can disguise the fact that plain English common-sense has prevailed in the end—and will prevail."

"Boyd Robson is quite right; we have not only

to realise our ideals, but insist upon others recognising them as correct." And Hilda Kewney folded her hands across her lap complacently.

"Then must the ideals they cannot be made to recognise be sacrificed in order to realise the others?" asked Beatrice sorrowfully.

"We will not sacrifice one," said Redhead.

"That's right! There must be no sign of weakness. By a lucky chance we have hit upon the right way of impressing the world through Snyder; that policy must be continued at all costs." And Sterry began to pace the room.

"The modern creed is comprised in the theory that the fittest to survive, survive. To my mind it is a perfectly hellish doctrine; but naturally, if we wish to impress those who believe it, we must show that we are very much alive. We will put other inventions on the market, attack other industries, and make a position for Cristallia."

"That will be to provoke further hostility. No nation troubles very much if one industry is snuffed out by foreign competition; but attack many simultaneously, and the policy of laissez faire will be quickly abandoned," objected Toller.

"What does that matter," asked Robson, "since we are to be suppressed?"

"Do you really believe that, Mr. Robson?" asked Madeline tearfully.

"Yes. Don't we all believe it? It is only a question of when. We must go, as all reformers before us have had to go. I do not see that we have any chance."

"Then why not by compromise lengthen our period of usefulness?" asked Toller persuasively.

"Because we cannot go back on our principles. They are right, and we are too much in earnest; it is our nature. That's why, Harry."

Sterry took Robson by the hand and grasped it warmly.

"That's right, Boyd. Thank you, our sentiments exactly. We'll not go back, whatever happens, but get as far ahead as we can in the time allowed us. What is it you want, Miss Bright?"

"A message from Fez. It seems important. Firbank has been told by Ahmed Fellalah that the German Emperor is to build a fort at Tangiers and give a battery of four Krupp guns in exchange for a concession in the Sus."

"All right. No answer."

"No sooner is any new thing a success than Germany makes a bad imitation," observed Redhead, screwing up his mouth.

"There! You said '*success*' Willie!" And Hilda Kewney's long arm, with index finger outstretched, reached right across the table towards the "chief commoner."

"Of course Cristallia is a success! And will be a much greater one soon," said Sterry, now quite enthusiastic again. "You take just whatever you want, Boyd, to make Cristallia strong both to repel and attack."

Robson got up and stretched himself, yawning; then, with a laugh, said:

"My fist is not so hard as John Bull's; I'll get some knuckle-dusters, I think."

Jones put up his hand and snapped his fingers.

"Iltydium's the thing for you. Why not make your cannon and shells of Iltydium—hardened with tungsten, you know?"

"I think I know something better than tungsten to harden Iltydium, Mr. Jones," said Beatrice Tyacke solemnly.

"You, Beatie! You don't know what Iltydium is."

"I think I do."

"Who told you? Name! name!"

"I found it out myself."

"Never! What is it?"

"Don't give the secret away, Beatie," said Hilda

Kewney, much amused, and passing a pencil and paper towards her.

The girl wrote a few words on a scrap, and handed it to Jones.

"You clever little woman! Who would have thought it? You're more than a genius, Beatie. I must have a talk with you. Come down to my laboratory. I can tell you something too. Come on, come on."

CHAPTER X.

THE DAY DREAMS OF A BUSINESS MAN.

HARRY TOLLER, who from the beginning had made himself responsible for the successful working of the commercial side of the Cristallian venture, was something more than a man of figures. To him, even the analysis of an elementary balance-sheet was a study in human nature, every item expressing some motive the secret of which he ought to discover. Therefore he had watched the growth of the colony with uncommon interest—an interest that amounted almost to passion—but he hid all that he felt behind that conventional mask of indifference which is the despair of the enthusiast, and his comrades scarcely knew that he was wholly one with themselves.

The cause of the attempted insurrection he could not understand; he himself was so thoroughly imbued with the perfection of their policy and methods that he was surprised any one living in Cristallia did not at once come wholly under its spell. To him the attitude of those who knew nothing of its inner working was comprehensible; the aloofness of those who did was not, and the disclosures Robson had made greatly disturbed him.

Harry Toller assumed that every one, at some period of his or her life, hopes to do some little thing which will leave the world better for the act being done. An optimist, he had that faith in mankind that fits one for life among a progressive people, and he firmly believed that in Cristallia all must come right because their motives were good.

Danger from outside he could understand; he expected attack, and thought that when the great struggle for supremacy came—and changes come quickly in this age of energy—Cristallia would be able to hold its own. Their little community had settled in the very darkest corner of Africa, a corner that is purposely kept dark by nations who were strong enough to have effected reforms, but lacked courage through mistrust of each other. It was unlikely that the Great Powers would view without concern the establishment of a new nation—one that sooner or later would threaten their supremacy on land or the seas. The stronger Cristallia became, the sooner would the struggle begin. As Spain in the sixteenth century tried to crush England because she entered into rivalry with Spain as a sea-power, so would the great manufacturing countries attempt to overthrow the new community which threatened their supremacy in their own special field.

For the rest, the civilisation of Cristallia was of another sort to that of which the world knew and most esteemed. The remarkable thing in its short career was the wondrous increase of wealth—of that material wealth the Isocrats counted worthless. Coined money from the first had no circulation in the colony; there was a paper currency, and the profits accruing from trade accumulated so rapidly it was difficult to find remunerative investments of the kind needed. The wants of the people were so few that the labour they rendered the State left always a credit balance in the favour of the worker. Fitzjoy hoped that gold would be discovered in the Atlas, and in the rush that would follow Cristallia's "Isocracy" might be swamped. He overlooked the fact that they had no need for gold; they could obtain more commodities in exchange for the labour they expended in producing Iltydium than they could for the same labour employed in quarrying and crushing quartz—the more plentiful gold became the less the purchasing power of labour; soon, for their own protection, they might be forced to hoard the metal in lieu of investing it.

In like manner their criterion of moral worth differed. To begin with, all were equal; there was no fictitious value assigned to birth—any one babe was as much, or as little, honoured as another. They esteemed more than the others only those men and women who invented means of lessening labour without decreasing the productiveness of their factories. Mere knowledge, exceptional skill, personal prowess were not regarded as deserving special distinction; the possessors of them might be envied by some of the less fortunate, but collectively the Isocrats rewarded only those who knew how to apply the advantages for the common good.

On the south side people could be found who would applaud the youth who ran a hundred yards in a fraction of a second less time than his mates, or cheer the veteran who, after long and arduous exercise, was able to balance a couple of billiard balls at the end of a cue on the tip of his nose, but the first exhibition of the Röntgen rays was the only thing that awakened the Isocrats to real enthusiasm in a whole twelve months.

In Cristallia extravagance in dress or demeanour excited only ridicule; the wearing of diamonds was tabooed particularly, and the number of native servants strictly limited. The whole régime was directed towards concentrating the superabundant energy within the domain of invention and research. All, as Boyd Robson said, were invention mad, and he was as insane as any one. It was more than a passing craze with them, although they admitted that its present fierce ardour could not long continue.

As the body is rested by varying the exercise, other intellectual work was used as a foil to the exhaustion of creative genius—it was satisfactory to the Isocrats if recreation were kept to the mental plane. They argued that the human body, by the elimination of the unfit in ages past, was practically perfect for such labours as their mode of living entailed; but, on the other hand, with abundant leisure from manual toil, the human intellect could be developed until genius should be the rule, not the exception, among their people.

Just as far-away New Zealand in a generation gone had by its very remoteness attracted only the wealthiest, sturdiest, and most persistent of colonists, so Cristallia, by placing a premium upon originality, expected to attract the finest and strongest intellects. So far removed were they from sympathy with the inane and frivolous, they seemed moral beyond temptation. Fitzjoy's expectation that the introduction of a half-dozen " merry she-devils " would lead to their downfall was foredoomed to failure. The antics of such only awakened amazement and disgust. That class could only thrive in that special pabulum provided by perverse living in overcrowded cities. Even the newest comer, a wiry smith from Daisy Bank, saw nothing inviting in their wiles. The water-melons he was growing were already "larger than the vegetable marrows in Tom Fisher's garden in Cradley"—a fact he thought more uncommon and interesting than the gyrations of the "merry she-devils," so he preferred to study the melons.

All that, as Toller knew, was in the past; now, as Robson had revealed, there was discontent, if not revolt, and he himself could attribute it only to the influx of new talent being greater than the power of the Isocrats to absorb. The growth of the colony had been too rapid; extensive pruning seemed an imperative necessity.

Personally, he objected to the spirit of Robson's

policy, though admitting the cogency of his reasoning, and he found an unexpected ally in Redhead, whom he had always considered thorough, relentless, and aggressive. To Sterry, whom Robson had quite won over, Redhead had spoken without hesitation, and had met his objections with the quaint quotation, "I fear thou'rt becoming weak-kneed, brother," at which reminder of "Honest Bob's" minister in days of Plainfield and the little Bethel Sterry now scowled.

The truth was that the community by becoming aggressive risked what little they had now, and to them all that little was very dear. Perched up in the "Crow's Nest," a small turret on the south-eastern corner of the terrace before the Capitol, Toller looked down upon the town, out to sea, or, turning, beheld the purple-topped summits of the Atlas range. The sun was just dipping into the azure water in the golden west; the hoarse murmur of the Mohammedans at prayer mingled with the distant roar of the inland torrent. All work in the fields and on the quays had ceased, and in the hour of rest Sterry, Robson, and Alan Winship were walking together on the terrace. From the earnest manner in which Robson was gesticulating it seemed that the usually taciturn contractor was now being listened to with interest. At the other end of the terrace Madeline Winship was strolling arm in arm with Beatrice Tyacke and Hilda Kewney. They too were engrossed in conversation, and, oddly enough, kept aloof from their co-Councillors. Toller watched them, and sighed; mayhap there were differences growing even within the inner circle.

But Cristallia as a whole, for which they were living, what would it become? He looked out towards the setting sun and was reminded of its sex, for there are people who fancy sex pervades all things create. To some even Mohammedanism seems the masculine counterpart of Christianity, and

G

Toller himself always thought of certain towns, districts, and nations, as being, some under the domination of one, as others under that of the other principle. To him, England, as a whole, was a masculine entity; the Celtic race was feminine. The Anglo-Saxon nation was masculine, as was the Roman race; Egypt particularly typical of the all-enduring, never-changing, eternal feminine.

He sat there long, considering what Cristallia would become. The short twilight passed, and the silvery moonbeams danced on the rippling water and cast a ghostly sheen about the Iltydium pinnacle on Cristal Point. The lights in the town were few, for the people were mostly out of doors; a breeze stirred the leaves of the trees on the terraces below, and, but for the solitary figure of some Moor guarding the approaches to the Capitol, the Isocrats on the terrace might have considered themselves the only inhabitants of the place. All was so peaceful, serene, and still, withal so beautiful and intense, that Toller was impressed with its feminine spirituality —of all colonies in Africa Cristallia alone embodied that principle.

The fancy pleased him; he thought this child of their creation less ephemeral, and more influential, than the blatant, roaring, aggressive communities of the south. Cristallia would endure when they were forgotten.

The solution of their present difficulties he conceived to be possible by restoring harmony in the Council. What was lacking he knew not; but clearly the old frankness that used to be common among the Isocrats existed no longer.

He looked down on to the terrace; the women were still promenading at the extreme end. The men had ceased talking, but were still walking up and down together. At last Robson left his companions and went to the other group. Sterry soon missed him; then he and Winship followed, and soon all stood together. Toller strained his eyes to see with whom it was Sterry was talking. He was the first to leave, and he went alone. A few seconds after, Madeline Winship left the terrace, taking the opposite direction, towards the town. Robson then walked across to a seat and lit a cigar, and Hilda Kewney came bustling along the terrace calling for Toller.

CHAPTER XI.

A BAPTISM OF FIRE.

ABOUT three months after Snyder had been taken prisoner on the Belgian packet an ill-spelled letter arrived in Cristallia from a mechanic in Denver who complained that the vacuum valve was his invention and had been stolen from him by a German immigrant named Hans Schneider. The letter was shown to Snyder, and he admitted its truth—there was no likelihood of an invention from him, not though they kept him imprisoned all his life. He had nothing in him. They kept him close all the same, and thus the industrial community became saddled with its first burden. Not that so little mattered at all; the place was growing rapidly, factories were springing up in all directions along the south shore, and what had once been the golden strand of the outer harbour was now a great shipbuilding yard.

The flags of Holland, Roumania, and Switzerland flew alongside that of Sweden near the Guest House; explosive works and Samuel Amber's new gum factory were in isolated parts of the backlands on the banks of the Cristal River; and there was a daily service of trains between Port Cristal and the great native mart at El-Aksa. Here and there on the high ground were suspicious-looking mounds which to the initiated might seem to mask hidden batteries. There was an open fort on the hill

A BAPTISM OF FIRE.

above the south quay, and on Cristal Point a huge pyramidal block of Iltydium, rising from its spiral pedestal an elongated hollow cone twice the height of the world's greatest monolith, by day glistening in the sun like the burnished point of some huge spear, and at night illuminated with an arc light, scattering bright rays over town and harbour.

The Isocrats had quite recovered from the fright their temerity in seizing Snyder had occasioned; all the same, they strengthened their defences. The foundations of the great school had been utilised to erect fine barracks, now occupied by five hundred Moors under Lukeeli. The only source of danger apparently was the newly established German trading factory at Wadi-waar, but that was experiencing the usual luck of German colonies—burning a lot of gunpowder, costing a heap of money, and peopled by British and American adventurers and the off-scouring of the Latin countries. As for the Belgians, they had given little trouble; a demand for an indemnity made on their behalf through Sweden and Ulitsen had been met with blank refusal by the Isocrats, so they tried diplomacy elsewhere, and went on building their gunboat. The Powers which guaranteed Belgian neutrality saw no reason why they should undertake a war to maintain the little prestige Belgium fancied she still possessed, and to all intents and purposes it seemed that the Snyder incident was settled.

But there was a disagreeable surprise in store for the Isocrats, and it developed with such suddenness that they could not avail themselves of the defences they had prepared. One day, at the beginning of winter, when Boyd Robson was at Krasnoe Zeloe showing the Russians the superiority of Iltydium shells over all others; when Lukeeli and half his Moors were at El-Aksa for the autumn fair; when the "Gleam" was at sea off Cape Verde trying to communicate with Cristallia by means of improved transmitters; when the Shereef's big cruisers "Crescent" and "Hadj" were cruising along the distant Riff coast; when every one in Cristallia was working, as unconscious of coming danger and as unsuspicious as usual, a warship was seen approaching from the north-west.

Luckily Morven Kell was in the harbour directing the work in the breakwater, and when the warning bells from the watch-tower rang through the town he assumed command. As arranged, the factories emptied, the fires were closed down, and all but the few men necessary to keep the ovens going went to their posts on the defences. On the trading side there was a slight panic, but pratique was immediately given to the funky ones, and in less than an hour three ships thronged with women, children, and the timorous put to sea for Agadir, Mogador, and Casa Blanca.

Some relief was felt when the Stars and Stripes were distinguished above the fighting-tops of the great cruiser; but the joy was short-lived. The vessel refused a pilot, manœuvred prettily in the roadstead, then steamed into the outer harbour. A steam pinnace was at once launched, and landed a lieutenant with despatches on the north quay, where a couple of hundred Moors were marshalled. The ship proved to be the new warship "Oklahoma," which had sailed from Battery Point ten days before with sealed orders, but, as was generally understood, to join the United States Mediterranean Squadron at Villefranche.

The despatches were most laconic: Admiral Sanders was instructed to bring away from Cristallia the American citizen John Albert Snyder, but if dead, occupy the town until full reparation for his seizure and imprisonment had been made; in case of resistance, to bombard Cristallia after allowing the usual notice to non-combatants.

The answer was given at once. "John Albert

A BAPTISM OF FIRE. 87

Snyder would not be released to America or any other country with which he claimed citizenship, he being a member of the Commonwealth of Cristallia. The Executive would admit the Admiral or any officer higher in rank than a lieutenant to an interview with the prisoner Snyder, and grant him and his guard a safe conduct. The Commonwealth in no circumstances would allow the Admiral to occupy the town, protested against his threat to bombard it, and at the same time required him to remove the 'Oklahoma' beyond the three-mile limit before sundown."

Admiral Sanders was a veteran whose brilliant record could neither be heightened nor tarnished by fighting Cristallia. He put etiquette aside and went ashore. Snyder was wild to get away, and besought the Admiral not to desert him. With the Isocrats the Admiral was frank to friendliness. He and Hanlan's father had been through the "shop" together; Sterry's father he knew by reputation; and he had no wish to force the colonists unduly; but his instructions were peremptory.

"He knows our secrets; we will not release him," said Redhead firmly.

"All the more reason why he should be free," retorted the Admiral.

Madeline Winship made a last application: Cristallia harmed none, Snyder had ruined many, his record should be shown the Admiral.

"Madam, I cannot look at it."

"Then you, with him, will war on us?"

"Not on you, madam; non-combatants will have ample time to reach safety."

"There are no non-combatants among Isocrats. We, men and women, have equal rights, equal duties. If you fire a shot at Cristallia, I shall be with the other women in the forts."

The Admiral shrugged his shoulders, and turned abruptly to the Chief Commoner.

"I give you until four o'clock this afternoon to bring Snyder alongside; if he is not there, I shall take what steps I think necessary to secure him."

Then Sterry spoke.

"We will allow you one hour to get outside the harbour; a pilot is at your disposal if you take him at once, otherwise——"

"I take no instructions from any one whom the United States Government does not officially recognise. No, sir."

"Then you may take it unofficially that we do not recognise any rules of war. You can gain your victory only by exterminating us."

"You may be glad that the United States Navy observes the rules of war usual among civilised nations; you will be glad of that after we have pounded at you for an hour or less. You know my terms."

"And you know ours. The 'Oklahoma' must be outside or at the bottom of our harbour at sundown."

When the Admiral with his guard reached the shore the harbour guardship lay alongside his pinnace and accompanied her to the outer harbour.

The pyramid and diagonal flag of Cristallia was run up at half a dozen different places on the heights above the forts and flew from the staff above the Capitol.

Morven Kell went out in one of the harbour "crabs" with gear to foul, cut off, or wedge fast the propellers of the foreign warship. She had not dropped her anchors, but was fitfully steaming ahead or astern to keep in the fairway against the outrunning tide, and it was unlikely he would accomplish anything.

From the conning-tower over the Capitol Redhead and Sterry watched the enemy clearing their vessel's deck for action, and below, in the instrument-room, Beatrice Tyacke was transmitting to New York and London the particulars of the quarrel and position

A BAPTISM OF FIRE. 89

of the opposing parties as dictated by Redhead into the telephone.

Four o'clock struck upon the great bell in the Capitol; the guardship glided back into the harbour, and the "Oklahoma" was swinging round rapidly in the narrow channel, when a message came from Kell, who had returned to the north shore, that he had fixed a pirbright-cutter against the starboard propeller shaft, and that elsewhere all was in readiness.

Then a puff of light smoke was seen on the steamer; it was followed by a dull roar, and the first shot fired at Cristallia broke into fragments on the rocks high above the town. At two minutes' interval it was followed by another, which expended itself as harmlessly.

There was no answer from any of the land forts, but in the outer harbour the water bubbled up and burst into a blaze which spread for a few yards, then died out and left a low hanging cloud of green smoke between the ship and the town. Before the next shot was fired the flame burst forth anew nearer the ship, and she was headed for the mouth of the channel, but another warning bubble to the port side led to the helm being sent hard over again. At three separate points the bubbles were now bursting into flame, and the fire was spreading over the surface of the water like burning oil. The guns were silent; the ship, swinging right round into the blaze and smoke, churned the water to muddy, smouldering froth, and then at top speed the "Oklahoma" rushed along the channel for the sea.

Before she escaped the burning water, with its low-hanging poisonous green cloud, a mine was fired, and suddenly a huge mound of flaming water fifty feet high and nearly a hundred yards in length rose right before her. Into the trough she plunged, pitched heavily but righted quickly and in time to ride the swelling sea in safety, but only to be caught by the rush of water from a wave equally formidable thrown up by a charge of five hundred pounds of gun-cotton submerged fifty yards to her right. By this wave the "Oklahoma" was thrown almost on to her beam ends to port and forced to the edge of the channel, but, admirably handled, she was headed round in time and kept afloat in the deep stream.

The bad steering that immediately followed indicated that one blade at least had been lost from the port propeller, and if the pirbright-cutter did its work the warship would soon be quite unmanageable. The water dripping from chains and cathead was here and there still aflame, burning slowly like sulphur, and on the great hull glowing patches of the devouring slime could be seen still adhering.

In a few minutes she reached the open sea, and was washed clean by the spray she threw to right and left. Then the guns were swung out again and the firing recommenced. She went to and fro in the roadstead, sending shell into the woods and on to the rocks above the town. The harbour was still bubbling up with the inflammable gas, and the smoke hung about the deserted quays and lower forts.

The Americans were expending their energy uselessly at sham fortifications, pounding solid rocks far removed from the men who were working the few guns which from time to time sent a shot at the fast-travelling ship.

Flag after flag disappeared on the rocks; the staff above the Capitol had been cut through with shot; and still besieged and besiegers fired at each other without cessation. Darkness was coming on; the tide had turned; far away to the west those on the watch-tower noticed that quickly growing speck in the sky which heralds a tropical storm. The vapour about the town thickened, and the order was sent to fire more carefully, as the "Oklahoma" apparently had not once been hit; then the firing from the forts flagged; became quite desultory as all shots were seen to strike wide.

Those on the ship noticed the indication of the coming storm, and their firing became more rapid; and the Isocrats on the watch-tower lost faith in the pirbright-cutter, and longed for the hurricane to strike their antagonists and for the darkness of night to hide themselves. It was not comforting to receive a message from the Hadj Larbi, their agent in Fez, that His Shereefian Highness would not interfere. The American Minister had arranged for his neutrality months before. The Isocrats must fight the battle out alone.

There was little chance of hitting the "Oklahoma" in the increasing darkness. She seemed to be drawing further off shore and to be making for Agadir when the storm struck her. For a few minutes she did well, and firing was suspended; then she swerved and lay helpless. The cutter had done its work at last; the starboard propeller had broken off, and, with the end of the shaft, was at the bottom of the sea. The "Oklahoma" was at their mercy now, and for the instant Sterry and Redhead were too overjoyed to send the order to cease firing.

Then Admiral Sanders did a plucky thing. The ship was headed for Port Cristal and driven slowly ahead before the storm. All her guns available were trained forward, and with a quick, raking fire from all arms she advanced towards the harbour.

The booming of the artillery, the incessant din of the machine-guns, the sharp rattle of the rifles prevented those on the ship observing that from Cristallia not a shot was now being fired. They knew only that they had to silence the forts and awe the garrison before they reached the harbour, and to gain this they spared no effort. The wind blew the floating flames towards the north shore, and up into the river; to continue that defence was therefore useless. Already the vapours, driven inland by the wind, hid the town and Capitol; only the south fort had an unobstructed view of ship and harbour. There the flag had gone, but, well screened from rifle fire, the men were lying watching the incoming ship, and a search ray brought them to the attention of the gunners. Soon shells were bursting over the open fort, while an incessant blind fusillade was continued against the town and both shores.

The great waves were rushing over the part-formed breakwater and the wind blew like a hurricane when the disabled ship, in trying to make her entrance of the harbour, struck a bank, swung round, headed off, turned again, drifted stem foremost against the breakwater, was forced full length upon it, and heeled over slowly.

The firing then ceased, and in the lull above the echoes reverberating from the hills could be heard wild cries of despair and pain from the town, where, in two different places, flames were bursting forth. Jake Hanlan, who had charge of the great gun, could contain himself no longer; with a few turns he lowered the elevation of his piece, already directed upon that part of the breakwater from which a cloud of white steam was issuing, and at once pulled the fuse. The bullet went home; they in the fort heard distinctly its fierce clash on the armour of the cruiser.

"Sink the devil there! She'll save a million skeps of concrete!" hissed Kell as the hydraulic lift brought the next shell into position.

Before it was rammed home in the gun a distress rocket shot up skyward from behind the driving cloud of steam, and then Madeline Winship rushed on to the gun-stage.

"No more, Morven, no more! We must save them!"

Jake Hanlan laughed; Kell looked puzzled. It was too absurd—with Cristallia in ruins and ablaze.

Jake laid the gun afresh and was feeling for the fuse, when another rocket went up from the ship.

"Stop! I command it! I take responsibility!"

The girl's face was very white, and she was trembling violently. Kell went towards her and would have supported her.

She understood his intention.

"No, no! leave me. Signal to the rocket station and order out the lifeboats! Quick! Quick! They must not perish!"

The wind caught her draperies and blew out her burnoose like a pennant in a storm; she struggled to keep her place; snatched at the breech-key of the gun, and missed; then was blown down on the floor of the fort into the arms of a couple of Moors. But she had gained her point. The gun was lowered, the signals raised, and the work of rescue began.

CHAPTER XII.

KNIGHTS OF THE BACK STAIRS.

"FERSTEN, those American friends of yours who are playing at empire-making in Africa have scored again." And the Honourable Benjamin Fitzjoy threw down a despatch and curled his lips disdainfully.

"The Isocrats?"

"The United States Government is pleased to recognise the industrial community of Cristallia as the African Commonwealth," he repeated, as though reading the words of the dispatch.

"Recognised their independence, eh? You will do the same?"

"I think not, Fersten. We might not object to a fresh dependency in Africa, but new independencies anywhere are quite outside our limit."

"Toller thinks the petition will be granted this time."

"Blessed are they who expect trustingly, for they shall long be kept waiting. But to come back: the rescue of those nine hundred Yankees was distinctly good. In lieu of treating them as prisoners of war, to send them home honourably was a master stroke of diplomacy. His loftiness the Chief Commoner of Cristallia is no fool, Fersten."

"Psh! It was not he!"

"No matter who did it, it was a lucky inspiration."

"Inspiration! There you have it; it was a woman's doing, of course, my friend."

"Don't you be too blessedly familiar, Fersten," said Fitzjoy, annoyed; then, swinging back in his chair, he put both feet on to the table to demonstrate his superiority.

"We understand human nature: would any man who was being worsted in a fight for life turn round on a sudden impulse and save his enemy from an unexpected misfortune? What do you think?"

"Never mind what I think: what do you know?"

"Hanlan, an American, was going to fire at the wreck, when Madeline Winship got before the muzzle of the loaded gun and stayed there until the rocket-lines were over the ship and the lifeboats alongside."

"All the same, Sterry and the others had to ratify her action."

"What else could they do when, to speak metaphorically, she stood before their guns until they did agree?"

"Confound the woman!"

"Ah! you do not know that one."

"Don't I!" And his face expressed a recollection that was as forcible as unpleasant. "It is my belief that if the Dutch Consul had not been killed the Yankees would have been given their ship back and the whole affair hushed up."

"That could not be, because they——"

"I listen to no arguments which may tend to alter my belief. What luck Cristallia has!—the very ship disabled herself at the most opportune moment for them."

"It is a way warships have."

"True. They are more uncertain than a horse's health. There is a chance for the modern poet to improve on Shakespeare's aphorism. All the same, the gods are on the side of Cristallia."

"That is superstitious of you. The Cristallians themselves disabled the 'Oklahoma.'"

"How do you know that?" asked Fitzjoy quickly and earnestly.

"They put new shafts and propellers to her before they made her over to the Sultan of Morocco."

"That's nothing," said Fitzjoy, again despondent. "But enough of this humbug. What about your German settlement?"

"Pieterland? We thought to make it a Congo, but it's only a second Cameroons."

The doleful tone of Fersten sent Fitzjoy into a reverie. This community of Cristallia was a quite unknown quantity, and it puzzled him to assign it the position of proper relative importance in the new British cosmos; for the ambitious young Under Secretary looked far ahead, and was in the habit of regarding matters that might come within the domain of practical politics when he attained the rank of Cabinet Minister. He examined all in turn, from the Alaskan frontier dispute to the occupation of Thursday Island, in order to discover the thing which, properly handled, might make a Premier of a Cabinet Minister. In the Morocco question he thought he had found a problem which would soon be ripe for solution.

"After all, they are only a handful of enthusiasts," he mused.

"The Pieterlanders?"

"No; the others. They must fall into line with the greatest empire the world has known, or be snuffed out."

"You may trust them to do the right thing," said Fersten cynically.

"That will make them formidable; but I hate cynicism in others, Fersten, and especially in you. It ill becomes an Isocrat, I fancy."

"But the unexpected always happens."

KNIGHTS OF THE BACK STAIRS.

"Only to those who *will* expect the improbable. You and I know better than believe that sham truth, Fersten."

"Like the people of Cristallia, we must make things happen, eh?"

"Have the Isocrats taken to that? An instance?"

"Germany put Jonesware on the list of prohibited imports: Cristallia at once retaliated by supplying Russia with Iltydium shells, and is to deliver to France the hull of a first-class line-of-battle ship, armoured with absolutely impenetrable plates. There's retaliation for you."

"Mere commonplace devices. I believed the Isocrats unconventional in all things; therefore, possibly dangerous. What is really their object—their policy?"

"To reform the world."

"There are so many ways; which do they prefer?"

"The right one, of course."

"You know what I mean, Fersten."

"And I think you understand mine. *They* will reform the world."

"Quot homines, tot sententiæ."

"Not in a simple matter of right and wrong. You see, I have my lesson well."

"I forgot you are an Isocrat. But you do not agree with them in everything."

"Isocrats do not agree in all things; the axiom you are expected to believe is that the world needs reform, and there is only one way—the way you believe to be the right one. Absolute independence of thought and full liberty of action, but, in Cristallia, it is Cristallia which is *the* means to obtain the reform, and there is coalition ad hoc."

"And you have subscribed to that?"

"Not at all. I have a plan of my own, quite antagonistic."

"You will have progress by antagonism, eh?"

"I do not know; I hope to make things happen."

H

"Crafty Fersten! You have a plan; but have you their confidence?"

"I helped von der Pfordten over that ugly Dutch Consul trouble; I am all right with them."

"And I helped you—don't forget that! I suppose you have not thought it necessary to inform What's-his-name of that fact; consequently, I may not be 'all right' with the Isocrats, as you say you are."

"I mean to make it pleasant all round. It is a question of terms."

"Undoubtedly."

"To wreck Cristallia every one is ready; secret service money is plentiful. Germany, Austria, Belgium, and—may I say——?"

"Say nothing if you are wise. I think we two understand each other perfectly, Baron Fersten."

The intriguer looked glum, and twirled his long moustachios; then he laughed blatantly.

"As though that were sufficient! Indicate——"

Fitzjoy shook his head with unusual vigour.

"Well, the money question apart, how shall I be received provided Cristallia falls and I have wed an Isocrat out there?"

"I suppose it will be the same as if the marriage were made at Malta. Who is the victim? The young woman who fronts the cannon?"

Fersten shook his head.

"I cannot risk refusal. There is another one who receives and transmits all the private messages for the Commonwealth. A neat enough little woman, Tyacke by name, and she alone among the women knows the secret of Iltydium and Jonesware."

"A valuable acquisition—when Cristallia is no more. I should certainly insist upon the marriage tie being binding, if I were you, Fersten."

"Not *after* I have the secrets—and am safe from Cristallia. But that is not the whole of my plan. I am going to introduce 'La Grande' to Cristallia."

"Irma the Magnificent? That Paris should lose

so much! Again I say they are lucky dogs in Cristallia."

"You know now how the chances stand. One thing only is needed to make success certain."

"Money?"

"I have more than enough. No; I want a really good invention. Something to divert suspicion. But you can't get one for love or money nowadays. Every one goes to Cristallia direct with new things. There isn't an invention worth a cent left in this country—or any other."

"What a relief! We always provide our own in the service. It is the better way since men have confidence in their own things. Besides, if the various departments could not give the country all it wants, public confidence in the personnel might be weakened. That reminds me; I will order the Admiralty to invent something better than these Iltydium shells and plates—that will aggravate the Isocrats."

"Not in the least. The Isocrats are born stoics one and all. Nothing would perturb them."

"They are dangerous people—snuff them out!"

"It is the only thing to do; we have come to that conclusion. They care for nothing civilisation can offer them; they are as untractable as people who have no fear of death. They must go."

"Luck to you, Fersten," said Fitzjoy, smiling grimly and stretching out his hand.

CHAPTER XIII.

"FOR THE FUTURE OF CRISTALLIA."

"BOB, what do you think of Fersten?"

"I think he is a 'rotter'! Look at the time he has been in getting his gum factory started! The humbug!"

"The delay is annoying; but there are circumstances." And Willie Redhead aped the manner of the Baron so closely that Sterry laughed at the mimicry. "Then Fersten is such a pleasant companion."

"The fellow is too plausible; one can't help liking him. But he is no good for Cristallia, Willie; his heart is not in the work."

"Because his heart is more drawn to one of us than to all."

"You mean the game he is carrying on with Beatrice Tyacke? I have noticed it, and I won't have that sort of thing from him."

"Why not? And how shall you stop it? Beatrice Tyacke, like the rest of us, is now free to wed whomsoever she may choose."

"As if Fersten meant it seriously. The man is simply a poseur!"

"But serious enough in this. You have been over the house he is building for himself at the factory?"

"I have; and I know that Fersten must produce his 'whalebone substitute' before he goes to live in that house. He has wasted time. We are no nearer an output from the factory than we were six weeks ago. I spoke with Fersten only to-day, and told him what I thought."

"How did he take it?"

"Quietly enough; said that he should have to go to Europe again. It is that makes me suspicious. This precious invention of his may be of the 'made in Germany' order after all; perhaps it is a put-up thing from one of the Government laboratories, and Fersten only a spy. You remember his attempt to get into the different factories—his absurd assumption that, being an Isocrat, he could go everywhere in Cristallia. I have watched him closely since then; and as he is going to Europe he must go at once. It will be his last chance. If he does not produce the real thing within a reasonable time after his return, I shall ask the Council to 'fire' him."

"But they cannot. Once an Isocrat, always an Isocrat."

"Yes, but when once in Cristallia, not there for ever. He can be made to leave the place for the common good."

"You think the Council will agree to that?"

"They must. I shall state the reasons; they will pronounce as a matter of form; and I shall see that effect is given to the resolution. You will not object?"

"Oh, I am only a useless figurehead."

"What nonsense! You are *the* authority on the quarterdeck; I am only a helmsman taking my 'trick' as do others. No, Willie, I thank my stars that the laying of the course does not devolve upon me. You are the brains of the concern, old boy!"

"Since you say so, then, I warn you that I see breakers ahead."

"How? Fersten knows nothing."

"Not that at all. Beatrice Tyacke may accept him."

"Whew! I had not thought of that."

"Will she have to go from Cristallia too?"

"Why go halfway to meet your troubles? Enough for the day is the evil thereof."

"That is like you. Will she have to go too?" he asked again.

His tone and look brought a reluctantly given answer.

"I suppose so—if the future of Cristallia should require it."

"Always the future of Cristallia." And Redhead sighed.

For the past three years that had been the shibboleth to which all Isocrats had bowed. It seemed that instead of forming a State which would free them to develop their own individual tendencies, they had created a monster and made themselves its slaves. They recognised this, but thought the restraint only temporary; some sacrifices had to be made in order to found an independent realm; but not always would the claims of Cristallia be so onerous. With the expiry of the term during which they had covenanted that none would marry they felt that the period of probation ended. The day passed, yet they hesitated to use their liberty—the claims of Cristallia were more potent than personal inclination.

The future of Cristallia preyed upon Willie Redhead more than upon his associates; to him the wellbeing of the State was as dear as life itself. He felt that it afforded him the one chance of impressing his personality upon the world and upon posterity. He saw with satisfaction that the mechanical inventions of Sterry and Iltyd Jones brought them renown and profit; but he wished not to be an inventor only, but aspired rather to become the founder of a higher civilisation. The inventions, the isocratic community Cristallia, were but means to that end; and whatever threatened one or all attacked him.

"FOR THE FUTURE OF CRISTALLIA." 103

The successes of the Isocrats in the limited industrial field they occupied excited only the envy of outsiders; Redhead's wish was to create a republic other nations would strive to emulate, and never was reformer so beset with difficulties. To guard against surprise and treachery, all work was carried on in isolated buildings, closely "tiled" as a Masonic lodge; their news messages were cryptographic cyphers none but the initiated could read, the instructions to the operators meaningless jargon to all who had not been personally trained at Cristallia; and yet they lived in fear that their secrets would be disclosed and the community ruined. The one hope was that some master invention would come into their possession, armed with which they would be strong enough to defy the great powers of the world. It was no idle dream. Since the bombardment they had expressed their readiness to receive and use inventions serviceable for military defence, and had been inundated with schemes and appliances for the destruction of invaders. New weapons of offence would be offered if they wanted them and could invent nothing for themselves. Willie Redhead thought that he himself could devise an engine which would render war impossible, or at least wholly unprofitable. But to keep the State intact required increasing vigilance. Every item of news that passed through their agency was brought to his cognisance; a thousand small matters of detail had his attention each day, for he dared not depute the work, so fearful was he that he should lose touch with some insignificant ramification of their great enterprise.

The preservation of their independence, though all-important, was not the greatest difficulty with which he had to contend. That, indeed, was essential to a feeling of absolute freedom necessary to the development of national sentiment. To inculcate right ideas, to instil a desire for progress, to awaken a spirit of optimism—not only in the individual but in the mass—seemed an almost hopeless task. Yet its accomplishment was necessary to the success of the Cristallia scheme, and there were indications that the labour of teaching had not been vainly expended. Already the workers bore themselves as though conscious of some superiority, sometimes betrayed a suggestion of strength latent. A crisis would quickly determine what progress, if any, had been made, but as yet the people had not had occasion to take common action hurriedly. Redhead knew better than persuade himself that the populace was imbued with an enthusiasm to struggle for the realisation of that life he himself sought; but he hoped, ere he died, to have unmistakable proofs that such a sentiment animated one and all at Cristallia. Then he wished to ensure such conditions as would perpetuate the policy which called forth all that was good in human nature, believing that an improved race might ultimately be produced, and with them a still higher civilisation prove possible.

The commercialisation of aim induced by the over-appreciation of successes in the domain of mechanical invention and discovery reacted beneficially upon the best minds in the community of Cristallia. Nowhere, at no time, was there so much spontaneity in the quest of solutions to the haunting problems of destiny and the purpose of all life, of human independence and obligation, and of the sources of inspiration to endeavour. Individuals tried to express the highest hopes and deepest thoughts of the questioning, audacious, but always baffled human spirit in its varied attempts to solve the mysteries of consciousness. Their efforts showed only the tragedy of existence: by no means, in no conditions, can the individual escape his fate. This obvious truth was obscured by multitudinous issues in the turmoil of founding and developing the ideal commonwealth. When the main difficulties to material progress had been overcome Redhead fondly imagined that in their improved circumstances one and all of them would be happier. Instead, the consciousness of successful achievement in one direction but quickened the appreciation of suffering, and now the worst, as the best, were bereft of that imperturbable content which may fill the soul of the all-round failure. The most harrowing miseries, like the rapturous joys of ecstasy, appertain to the psychic identity and are eternal; for human ills Cristallia had no panacea, and only an optimist, such as Redhead, had faith to hope that an autocracy of thinkers might discover the remedy. True, in their community none suffered from the agonising primal claims of hunger; the workers had their full reward for bodily toil and were conscious of it; each and every one had the means to satisfy the demands of appetite and so master it; but, in the fuller, deeper life opened to most were harder trials and sharper pains. The fact was brought directly home to Redhead when one day, prior to the expiry of the covenant, he jocularly remarked to Madeline Winship that Robson had expressed his satisfaction that the term was so near its end.

"Poor Boyd!" said Madeline.

"Poor?"

"Poor because I fear he will wish that 'liberation day' had not arrived—and never would come. Pray God he may be the only one!"

Then Redhead understood: uncertainty was preferable to the hopelessness of unrequited love, and if Robson would be disappointed, then Madeline certainly had her own troubles. "And to think Bob is so blind as not to see that the girl is not sacrificing all for us, but for Cristallia, because Cristallia is his," said Redhead to himself; and he looked at Madeline questioningly without obtaining any confirmation of his suspicion. He assumed his optimistic mood and declared that in Cristallia every one must and should be happy, but Madeline only sighed and muttered something about reverting to the state of contentment in simplicity lived by Diogenes in his tub. Redhead, who had been so engrossed with inventions and schemes, and the questions of the day, had not troubled to observe closely any but Sterry, who by no sign or word betrayed any feeling he might at any time have entertained for one of his associates. Now that Redhead was anxious for information as to who would marry whom he could gather but little. In their free converse with each other the Isocrats usually called one another by their Christian names, but occasionally the more stilted form of address was heard, and this led Redhead to suppose that when, for instance, Beatrice Tyacke called Madeline's brother "Mr. Winship" there was present an excess of feeling which prevented familiarity, and hence recourse to the old conventionality. So, to Robson, Madeline was always "Miss Winship," but he was simply "Boyd" to her. This was but a trifling indication and not wholly applicable, for Iltyd Jones, Hilda Kewney, and Jake Hanlan remembered only the surnames of anybody when they themselves were angered.

Redhead wished that all would settle down happily, and became anxious. If Robson were rejected, he might wander away into the wilderness; Alan Winship, disappointed, might throw up the agency work and rush off to Klondyke. Defections such as these—nothing in a great State—were appalling in a small community where, in short, the law of averages did not obtain, and nothing could be predicated from past experience.

Some few days after Fersten's departure there was an experimental demonstration of fort defences on the frontier, and to watch the results closely, all available leaders left the town. There remained only Iltyd Jones in full charge, and Beatrice Tyacke in the control of the news department. As luck had it, then the marriage question arose.

Iltyd, Deputy Chief Commoner for the time being, left his factories to the underlings, allowed State matters to drift, and, true to his métier, was dabbling to his heart's content with chemical mixtures in a private laboratory when Beatrice Tyacke abruptly entered.

"Mr. Jones, what answer am I to send to Mr. Fersten, who has just asked my hand in marriage?"

"Wait a bit, Beatie," answered Jones, whose attention was quite absorbed in watching a test tube and noting the rising register of a pyrometer in a closed furnace. "What is it? A special message—from whom?"

"Mr. Fersten," repeated the girl in a tone of disgust.

"That bounder! What does he want?"

"Me, I suppose."

"By the Sterrygraph! He can't have you. We haven't got that far yet. Now, watch this. Come here."

The girl still kept her hand upon the door.

"But he can have his answer."

"How?"

"I can promise."

"O Beatie, you won't—you can't—you mustn't!"

"But why not?"

"A hundred reasons. Don't you know all about Iltydium, and the adamant alloy—and all my secrets?"

"But is that a reason? I thought perhaps there was some rule which——"

"Oh, that's exploded. We are all free."

"Then I may——"

"I did not say so. It's an open question. Put him off until Willie gets back."

"I can't do that. It would be undignified. Am I not free?"

"Oh well, if you're free, do as you like; that is logical."

"But I do not want to do anything which would injure the Commonwealth."

"That is too good of you, but is it sensible?"

"Well, what do you advise? Is there no other way out?"

"There is, Beatie, there is. Marry me!"

"O Mr. Jones, do please be serious."

"For seriousness there is nothing like Iltydium—I mean Iltyd. Now, Beatie, just listen——"

"Not unless you will be serious."

"Am I not in earnest? Do I not look sober as a judge, solemn as the Chief Commoner of the greatest Commonwealth? What more can you want?"

"I want to hear sense. Can I say 'Yes' to Mr. Fersten?"

"You can—that is, you may; but I do not advise it. Oh, why was I let in for all this? What are you going to do?"

"I am going to take the responsibility, if you will not. You will make a memorandum that the application was made, please, Mr. Jones."

She went away quietly, and Jones took up the test tube only to put it down again immediately. It would never do for Mr. Fersten to learn all that Beatrice Tyacke knew about his inventions; and he sat down to puzzle out what ought to be done.

CHAPTER XIV.

UNWELCOME VISITORS.

"BOYD, I do not see how you can blame Fersten for the last raid. He has been in Europe for the past two months."

"That is true enough, Miss Winship, but he provoked the raid all the same, and had he been here it would have been more formidable. The Berbers are mad against us all since Fersten went over the Draa with his shooting party."

"As likely as not we get blamed for what the Pieterlanders do," remarked Sterry unconcernedly.

"Too often. We are all foreigners to the natives, who make no fine distinctions; but *I* hold that Fersten is clearly to blame for this last incursion."

"He'll soon be back. Let him settle the thing for himself." And Sterry showed that he was anxious for the next business.

"Not I. Fersten would soon have all the Atlas out against us; if he is coming back, we must keep him in town. When is he due?"

"By the next Marseilles steamer," said Redhead.

"What is the meaning of that? Why not by one of our own boats?"

"I think I can explain it," said Redhead quickly, and with the air of one who has news of importance to communicate. "He is bringing Irma de Meysembourg with him."

"The traitor! She must not be allowed to land."

"Why not, Boyd?" asked Madeline earnestly, and glancing from one to the other as though to learn their opinion.

"You do not know who she is!"

"The most notorious female in Europe," volunteered Hawkins, a staid, portly man of fifty, who had recently been admitted to the Council.

"To bring *her* is a direct insult to Beatrice and to us," returned Boyd hotly.

"Beatrice won't mind. I assure you that since she declined Fersten's offer she has no more interest in him than any of us have."

"You have her confidence," muttered Boyd, somewhat appeased.

Madeline nodded. "Then, as to ourselves, surely we are not so good that we must refuse a visit from even notorious people. I thought the old Pharisaical spirit had quite died out."

"Madeline is quite right, Boyd," said Sterry cheerily. "Fersten makes himself responsible for her conduct while here, and if she misbehaves, we can pack her off and have another excuse for firing him."

Boyd Robson shrugged his shoulders, but made no further opposition, and Kell grinned sympathetically.

"Then," said Redhead, "as to this proposed visit from the Princess of Andorra and the Prince Clovis of Calamine. We can't refuse, I suppose?"

"More humbugs," growled Boyd.

"What I want to know is, who asked them to come?" demanded Hilda Kewney.

"As yet, no one. Their Highnesses have merely intimated that they would not refuse an invitation."

"In other words," interrupted Sterry, "they've put old Ulitsen up to ask for one."

"The way common to porphyrogenetical parasites," growled Boyd.

Redhead ignored the interruptions.

"They are cruising incognito; have been to Cape Juby, and Grand Canary, and——"

"And Pieterstadt," interrupted Boyd.

"——elsewhere, on board the Prince of Monaco's yacht."

"We won't have Monaco here," surlily interjaculated Boyd.

"Not Monaco—only the yacht," remarked Sterry.

"All the same, there's a gambling-table on board."

"Surely we are proof against all temptations to roulette." And Madeline smiled.

"Quite right, madam, and I have no doubt but Cristallia can entertain these distinguished persons royally," sententiously observed Hawkins. "We are not savages, and know how to treat even—[what did you call 'em?]—parasites fittingly." And he looked at Boyd as though he had scored for once.

"That be hanged!" observed Sterry; "we shall make no distinction. If the royalties like to take us as we are, they may come and see us. We are all behind with our deliveries, and can waste no energies upon triumphal arches, decorations, or festivities."

"In short, they must take 'pot-luck,'" said Redhead.

"That's it; you have the sense of the Council; put it into diplomatic jargon, and the business is finished."

"We shall give them a guard of honour, of course. Moors, or our own men?" asked Hawkins.

"Neither—not a black even," said Robson emphatically.

"Really, Boyd, you are too uncompromising," said Madeline reprovingly.

"A few Moors, Boyd?" pleaded Hilda.

"Then, drat me! that other woman shall have a guard too. I'll be even with them somehow."

"Don't be ridiculous, Boyd," said Madeline.

"It's all ridiculous; the greatest tomfoolery we've undertaken since we started Cristallia. We must do the thing on European lines entirely or stick strictly to our own. Any middle course would make us the laughing-stock of our visitors and our people. Make old Van Oppen master of ceremonies, if you like, and go in for punctilious kow-towing. They are proficient in the art at the Hague, but I doubt if our people will stand it or could do the thing decently." And he looked sarcastically at Hawkins.

"Oh, there must be a guard," repeated that individual unabashed, and the proposition was generally echoed.

"Then I resign."

"Oh no, you won't, Boyd," said Sterry coaxingly. "Go off to El-Aksa until they have gone, if you like. Better stay and see us through."

"I should think so. It's only the beginning of mischief."

"We must make a fair show," simpered Hawkins, addressing himself to Hilda particularly.

"Then I'll send a message to Maraksh and get the Sultan to let the fleet call here."

"No, Boyd, please don't do that," said Madeline much in earnest.

"Why not? Let the beggars know there is some fighting strength within call."

"It will spoil the impression I want Cristallia to make," said Madeline.

"Let Boyd have his way in something, Madeline," interrupted Redhead authoritatively.

"But——"

"I know—I know; we will make them feel that Cristallia is beyond their attainment."

"I won't say anything more, but it would be a change these royalties might appreciate if for a few days in a foreign country they could forget there are such things as fleets and armies." And she looked at Boyd, hoping he might relent.

"They sha'n't over-enjoy themselves here," blurted the staunch upholder of the Commonwealth. "It will be rest enough for them to discard Court etiquette and Court dress for a time."

In such manner did the introduction of elements almost effete in old-established nations affect the Isocrats. Mayhap the trivialities which it had irritated some of them to discuss obscured the real purpose at issue. Of Fersten's scheme they were quite ignorant, and they could not know that the Courts of Europe were intent upon the conquest of Cristallia in their own fashion. The call of the cruising yacht was not unpremeditated; the voyage was the outcome of many consultations among crowned heads and had been the topic of innumerable royal missives. When the "dear cousins" were in accord as to who should be sent, the details were not easy of settlement, for the plan evolved as great strategy as a long campaign. The need was pressing. Heaven, from whence came all good things, had bestowed a princess royal too many, for whom a position had to be created. The big prizes and the little prizes duly apportioned, the unfortunate Princess of Andorra was without a king or a kingdom, and almost without hope. And the members of the royal race, being astute, knew that every defection from their ranks—as when some atavistic scion escapes the purple and attains the limited freedom of an aristocrat—is a loss of regal prestige, therefore to be guarded against. Numerically royalties increase, but their kingdoms decrease; only recently the German princelet to whom the Princess Andorra's elder sister was married died without issue, and his title and territory passed, by the action of the Salic law, into the all-devouring maw of Prussia. If matters were so, what was the outlook of the royalties of the next generation? Cristallia was a wealthy and prosperous community with unlimited possibilities; a chance of becoming a powerful

I

kingdom if rightly fostered, and even now, if as represented, a welcome consolation prize to the Princess Andorra.

Now, kings and queens and princes and princesses are, as all the world knows, ruled to some extent by their ministers, but in all that pertains to the royal prerogative they fight for their own hands as gamely as their ancestors warred on behalf of their people. To maintain their supremacy, to ensure their inheritance, their struggle is as arduous as that of the little draper battling against trade competitors—a common trait that makes the whole world kin. The prince and princess sent to Cristallia were as well equipped as training and foresight could make them, and they understood what was required of them—win they must. Ministers and statesmen, being less courtiers than aforetime, were fully occupied with their own intrigues, and whatever the Courts thought of Cristallia for their own family interests seemed very secondary indeed to the interests of States, so much so as to be regarded as a *quantité negligeable*. Thus it came about that the enterprises of which Fersten and the Princess Andorra were the exponents clashed disastrously, just as the arrival of both parties at Cristallia coincided.

The first advantage was with Fersten. No sooner did he see the royal yacht than he guessed the mission of the tourists. A hint to Irma was sufficient to put that leader of fashion on her mettle—never, Fersten declared, had she appeared so beauteous.

The mild, amiable, degenerate little Prince was in a quandary. He had availed himself of Van Oppen's company at Pieterstadt—for the worthy Consul did double duty—but the ceremonious official could give the Prince little advice worth having. He did not know, as a matter of fact, what procedure would be observed on the royal arrival or during their sojourn—it would be different from anything in Europe or anywhere else. Than Van Oppen none was better informed; the Prince must decide for himself and his suite. So, if there would be no getting into and out of various uniforms, and dashing hither and thither to make calls and leave cards, there was the worse difficulty—what to wear! He would observe his incognito—be simply the Graf von Esbach; but even then should his dress ape that of a waiter or one of the deck hands? It was a brain-racking problem. Much depended upon making a good impression from the first. In despair he determined not to change—but to go ashore just as he was; and so was wise by accident.

Van Oppen could suggest nothing for him or the Princess to do: there was not a hospital to open, nor a charity bazaar at which to preside, not a fund to which he could give; no poor, no schools, no mission, no churches—no call for a prince at all.

As ill-luck had it, the yacht and the French steamer arrived together. Van Oppen saw Fersten and the Meysembourg ferried to the north quay, while prince and princess remained on their yacht, undecided whether to land before the Guest House, like ordinary visitors, or await the call of some official. Van Oppen counselled them to wait, and told them of the Meysembourg's unexpected arrival.

"How will they receive her?" asked the Prince.

"Not at all. It is shocking. They must slam the door in her face. Really, she cannot stay in Cristallia the night; and at least, your Highness, you will sleep on board your yacht."

CHAPTER XV.

A "POT-LUCK."

"I SUPPOSE those plaguey wearers of the purple expect me to go aboard and fetch them instead of coming ashore like ordinary folk," grumbled Boyd Robson, to whose lot it had fallen to meet the visitors, and who had spoiled his temper by wasting half an hour on the quay.

When the yacht was snugly moored to the buoys in mid-stream he signalled Kell, who, in the harbour pinnace, had unostentatiously given the yacht a lead from the roadstead.

"Put me on board, Morven."

They sat opposite each other in the stern sheets silent as usual, but each knowing exactly the temper of the other, and each face reflecting exactly the other's emotion.

"The crew?" ejaculated Kell, as the pinnace neared the yacht.

"Give them a feed at the Guest House. Tell old Baillé to do the thing well, and you see the varmints don't loiter about the quays."

Robson had not the appearance of a commander-in-chief; but for the speckless condition of his clothes he might have been taken for a stevedore from one of the vessels loading at the quay. The pilot told

A "POT-LUCK."

the captain the rank of the visitor, and he, with due ceremony, presented Robson to Baron von Esbach. Very bluntly he bade the Prince welcome to Cristallia; then asked:

"Do you think Her Highness would like a guard of honour to escort her to the Capitol?"

The Prince was so well versed in the niceties of language that he answered without an instant's hesitation. Other commanders-in-chief would be offended if an escort were declined; this one's wish was made clear by his demand as to whether Her Highness would "like" instead of "accept." Evidently there was no escort at hand. "Her Highness was delighted to dispense with the services of a guard of honour. She felt quite safe at Cristallia."

"Then we'll go ashore," said Robson.

There was very little ceremony, but Robson and Kell between them got the company landed comfortably and quickly, and as the boats neared the steps a saloon waggon glided out from the cool shade of a tree-screened cavern and drew up on the almost deserted quay. The Princess and her suite entered and Robson followed; then the driver of the motor started for the Capitol.

"Even a railway cutting can be charming," said the Princess to Robson, admiring the dingles through which the car ran to reach the Capitol level.

"It depends who makes it," returned Robson ungraciously. But the Princess would not be offended, and talked with him about his contracting work and the railways her "royal cousin" the Duke of Nassau was making on his newly acquired territory. By the time the car reached the Capitol Robson thought the Princess a quite charming little woman. As for the Prince, he could even put up with him; he forgot "to be condescending," he explained to Kell.

So far from the door of the Capitol being closed to Irma de Meysembourg, she appeared to be a welcome visitor. She was with Sterry in the reception hall, and he had to be called repeatedly before he gave any heed to the arrival of the royal suite.

The Honourable Miss Hamilton, who possessed a keen eye for the proprieties, was the first to notice the Meysembourg's presence, and notified her disapprobation by raising her eyebrows and staring hard at the Comtesse de Gouvy. That lady promptly nudged the Prince, and he, in low tones, quickly apprised the Princess that she was to be Duchess of Melreux for the time being. It would never do for the Meysembourg to boast in Paris that she had met, possibly dined with, the Princess of Andorra, but the Duchess of Melreux had no reputation to maintain. The Princess acquiesced, but felt at a disadvantage. She was a dumpty, rather coarse-featured, unprepossessing creature who needed a full consciousness of regal ancestry to lend to her short stature even that pertness of bearing which did duty for dignity.

Nature had been more liberal of favours to Irma, the neglected child of an unknown father and nameless mother. She had been rightly nicknamed "The Magnificent," for her beauty was faultless. True, a Parisian superchic had declared that her ears were "heavy," but the faculty were against him, as he learned to his cost when a Court solemnly fined him for speaking derogatorily on a matter upon which only the leading anatomists were qualified to deliver an opinion. Her hair also was red, but in that particular she changed according to her own fancy or that of her admirers. Irma stood five feet nine inches in her stockings—a good foot taller than the Princess—and was every inch a queen.

Redhead did the honours thoroughly, and the Prince was amiable to friendliness. The Chief Commoner apologised that they could not show their factories; and the Prince answered that when on a visit to Berlin he did not expect to be shown the archives of the Prussian Chancelry—"and it is in your factories you are making history." Redhead explained that there would be no records for the future historians. "Our antiquated models we invariably destroy, of every discarded process we obliterate every trace; the inventors who discover what we once did will need to work out every improvement for themselves, and with the exception of Sterry and myself there is not a man living who could make the transmitters and receivers we first devised, nor any who could use them if they did." The Prince thought that an excellent policy.

There was a banquet in the evening, at which the foreign Consuls and heads of the departments were present. It was as dull as state affairs usually are. The next day Sterry, Jones, and half a dozen others had lunch on the yacht, and the Prince discussed with Sterry all topics save politics and the true object of their visit to Cristallia.

The Meysembourg was not to be thrust aside; she was ever with or seeking "Mon Bobbie"; told him in a hundred ways that she loved him, and kept repeating it in three words. She adored Cristallia, was tired of Europe, had cancelled her tour to the East, and wanted only to marry Bobbie and live within the "Palace."

The evening of the second day the Prince discreetly let it be known that he and the Princess would accept a "pot-luck" in the Capitol on the morrow. Like the American "surprise-parties," "pot-lucks" are right enough when the name is not taken literally; moreover, they were just then the fashion in Paris; and as the Prince and Princess wished to see the ordinary everyday life of the Isocrats, the "pot-luck" gave the opportunity.

At midday the Prince, with his chaplain, the Princess and the Comtesse de Gouvy, arrived at the Capitol.

"It is your wish that we observe no formalities,

Prince," called Redhead cheerily as his chair wheeled into the saloon.

The Prince bowed.

"None whatever, if you please, Monsieur le Président."

"All right, then, come along, sit where you like, with whom you will." And his chair rolled silently along towards the mess-room.

The Prince looked round somewhat bewildered, caught a glimpse of Mrs. Hawkins, but in advancing towards her collided with the ubiquitous Hilda Kewney, and apologising, escorted her to the table. The priest, divining the royal intention, offered his own arm to Mrs. Hawkins. Hawkins, at a loss what to do without his better half—for it was the one rule obligatory that husband and wife should sit side by side—hastily bowed to Beatrice Tyacke, and with a prodigious flourish hooked his elbow.

"It is as per usual, Miss Tyacke?"

"With pleasure; but pray be as usual, or we shall be disastrously ridiculous."

He dragged her away close upon the heels of his wife. Sterry saw Madeline, and joined arms with her—at which she was delighted. Fersten, arriving with the Meysembourg, noticed this and hastily followed, hoping for the next seat; but Iltyd, summoning courage, defeated him by interposing with the Comtesse de Gouvy.

"Aren't you going to get anything to eat, Princess?" asked Hanlan unceremoniously on his way through the room.

She laughingly answered that she hoped she was.

"Come along, then." And he grasped her arm above the elbow familiarly.

"Opposite the Meysembourg, please," she whispered.

"This is where you want to be, eh? Now, Morven, you just get over to the other side, will you? Thanks."

Robson, coming in late, drew out a chair and wedged himself in between Kell and the chaplain with less ceremony than a stranger at a farmers' "ordinary."

"Why do none of the ladies wear earrings?" asked the Princess.

"For the same reason they don't wear nose-studs or lip-buttons, I guess. We aren't barbarians, you know," answered Hanlan.

"And you think I am a barbaric survival?"

"If you like to take it that way, Princess."

"And I don't see any jewellery, although Monsieur Fersten said you made diamonds in the factories."

"Oh, Fersten's a dolgarned fool; aren't you, Fersten?"

Fersten bowed, spread his moustache, and smiled urbanely; but there was a momentary gleam from his eyes that Hanlan failed to notice.

"To talk about diamonds, when he can't make whalebone!" Words failed Hanlan to express the contempt he felt, but his tone adequately conveyed his meaning.

"I want you to talk about diamonds. Are they tabu in Cristallia?"

"We don't wear them on principle. Every stone means three months in a wire cage, endless drinks, and forced labour underground for some wretched nigger; diamonds aren't worth that price to Cristallia."

"But mine are not African diamonds; they were brought to Europe by Pizarro ages ago."

"I don't know that that alters the case; at any rate, Pizarro's name is not engraved on our Golden Scroll of Honour. I tell you what to do, Princess— sell your diamonds or give them away while they are worth something. We shall cheapen diamonds before we are through with our perchloride experiments, and when the 'slump' comes I hope all the others will be in the hands of Jews."

Out on the North Terrace, in the shade, the Prince found his opportunity of talking with Redhead as to the prospects of Cristallia. In the continued success of the colony he professed great interest.

"It is very clever—wonderful—for amateurs to have accomplished so much."

"We are practical," observed Redhead.

"Still amateur; you have not been trained from infancy in the art of government."

"Instead, we have learned to govern ourselves."

"Excellent. With professional aid you could accomplish so very much more."

"And lose our independence."

"Not in the least. Individually, you would possess greater freedom. Like Andorra and Calamine, a separate existence would be assured: at present Cristallia may be swallowed up by any big neighbour."

"Let the big neighbour try it," said Redhead contemptuously.

"A constitutional monarchy is the best form of government. The English know that, and they are a practical and free people."

"Deluded idiots!"

"A great nation. Cristallia may become a great nation as a monarchy."

"And a greater as a commonwealth."

"What was Calamine? What was Andorra? Pitiable the condition of struggling republics. Our house befriended them: they are now impregnable."

"As Monaco?"

The Prince bowed. "They are well governed, 'by the people, for the people,' as they were before. Their connection with our house has confirmed their government in the eyes of the civilised world. Through us they have become articulate; their voices are heard; they cannot die. Why do not you become King of Cristallia?"

"Because, Prince, I was reared a Republican and shall die one."

"Then it is impossible for you; but your friend Sterry?"

"Must answer for himself. We govern to the best of our ability, and our people are satisfied."

"Perfectly, I know, but the constitutional monarch does not govern; he reigns, which is a very different thing—much more easy and pleasant."

"Like the rôle of a British aristocrat."

"I am a warm admirer of the British aristocracy, but lords are not quite regal."

"Imbued with the same principles. They are grab-alls. Their forefathers seized the land, and their class held it until through their lack of government, or their bad government, the land became valueless. Then they seized upon the railways, canals, shipping companies, mines, and will hold them until they make them as unremunerative as is the land. The titled directors of companies have got the staple industries of Britain into their grasp, and they will not let go until by their incompetence they have ruined English manufactures. That must happen unless—unless the labouring class is elevated into what is now the middle class, when, having no class to look down upon, they will determine to have no class to look up to, and will sweep away the aristocracy and royalty in one great wave of revolution. The political position in Great Britain is most critical. Thank Heaven, we in Cristallia have no problem so difficult of solution!"

"But what is the religion of Cristallia?" asked Irma impatiently.

"Mohammedanism, I think," answered Fersten cynically; "but ask the Chief Commoner—he'll know."

In the silence that followed this outburst the Princess was heard to whisper, "Oh, why did I not ask that?" and for the first time since luncheon the priest gave evidence of being awake.

"Yes, what is our religion, Willie?" called Robson loudly.

"Mine is a modified Pantheism," answered Redhead somewhat amused.

"And mine the Protestant Church of England," said Hawkins boldly.

"Yes," remarked his wife complacently, "for fifteen years we never once missed attending St. Matthias's in the Camberwell Road, did we Joe?"

"No, my dear, most regular," he added, with a look round at all, which encouraged the Passionist Father to sidle up and commence a conversation on Anglican ritual.

"Why did you ask, Irma?" demanded Sterry, crossing over to her.

"Because I wanted to know, simpleton! I cannot believe Fersten; he is a deceiver. Tell me, Bobbie, can you make me Queen of Cristallia?"

"You?"

"Me—or any one?"

"Of course not."

"Then you are a deceiver too. I thought you were a man who could make anything. And if your wife is to be Queen, she must be one in her own right, eh? Say!"

"What nonsense!"

"I know, monsieur—I know well—you will marry that little thing over there! But you will deceive yourself; the Princess of Andorra will not reign here: Fersten will make me Queen of Cristallia yet; he has promised it."

"Very good of him, I am sure. Tell me all about it." And he led her aside.

CHAPTER XVI.

STRANGE IDOLS.

"THERE, Monsieur Hanlan," said the Princess of Andorra, "I repeat, not a sword in all Cristallia; yet you all, and always, carry firearms."

"You have been reading fiction, Princess."

"Ah no; it is true, is it not?"

"Who told you that rigmarole?"

"Baron Fersten."

"Baron!"

The Princess remembered; without betraying the slip by the least change of colour or voice, she covered the error.

"I call him Baron—he has the air distingué."

"Oh, that's what's the matter with him?" And Hanlan looked over at the spy.

"And you have a pistol in your hip-pocket?"

"What's the use of a gun in your hip-pocket unless you want to shoot a man behind you? I carry one in every pocket, and down a man while he's fumbling for his gun. I tell you what it is, Princess—never sleep with a pistol under your pillow, get it down in bed with you. I was out west when two Chinamen burgled the caboose. One stood at the head of my bed with an axe ready lifted to brain me if I stirred. His breathing woke me, when I saw the other

Johnny rummaging my grip. I pulled trigger on him, and he fell dead. The bed was on fire; and the other fellow vamoosed, taking the axe with him. Never you show your gun when you are going to fire."

" Show me how it is done."

" What shall I shoot at? I daren't kill a Moor; I'll ask the Chief Commoner if you can have a black."

" Oh no, no! Shoot at anything dead."

" Spoil new togs for nothing! Not me! "

" I'll mend the clothes. I suppose you think a princess can do nothing useful that way?"

" All right. A bargain! " He bowed, and removed his fez. " Which pocket? "

" The left-hand trouser pocket."

" The fez went high into the air; before it fell upon the terrace the report of a pistol-shot was heard, and the graze of a bullet seen upon the paving. A Moor picked up a tiny wad of red felt from the fez and presented it to the Princess.

" Bring me the cap. I must mend it."

" Excuse me, Princess, the fez is worth only a ' quarter,' and these are ten-dollar pants, new from the store to-day. I want 'em patched up, please."

The company gathered close round. Mr. and Mrs. Hawkins by brows and eyes held silent converse. Hanlan, laughing, turned away.

" Oh, Mr. Sterry, have you *no* rational amusements in Cristallia? Do you never dance? Do none of you take a hand at cards? " pleaded the Princess.

The Prince muttered something about the roulette-table on the yacht; then Madeline quickly suggested a visit to the Temple of Science.

To the grand hall in the northern quadrangle they went gaily, Sterry explaining to the Prince that it contained just the toys made by themselves for their own amusement.

The volimeter was the first instrument seen. A small delicately poised needle suspended in vacuo by a gossamer thread within a crystal dome. Below was a dial like the face of a clock. Simply by willing the needle-point could be depressed towards any figure; only the Chief Commoner could control its movements so absolutely that it pointed to each of the figures in succession.

"That is the automatic elector by which the future presidents are to be appointed," laughed Sterry. "That Redhead was elected before the toy was made proves how wisely we acted."

"Wonderful!" remarked the Prince, after trying ineffectually to control the needle.

"It is a French invention, not ours: there are a dozen like instruments in Paris and twice as many in London. None so delicate as this one, perhaps, still useful workable models. Do you understand the Kabbala?"

The Prince intimated that he did not, and asked where the flight of stairs before them led, and the meaning of the symbols over the door.

"That is the entrance to the lethal hall, the Temple of the Great Mystery, from which, having once entered, there is no escape. Lately we have affixed a self-acting mechanism to the 'soul-indicator,' and the door now will not open to any but the good. As you do not understand the value of mystic symbols, I may explain. There is a proper instrument working in that alcove, but this model, which you can see more comfortably, will serve my purpose. Within this crystal globe interlaced triangles float apparently upon nothing, but are really supported by what I may term 'soul-substance.' The pentagram is of the rarest of metals, the circlet of platinum. Before the instrument is this bar of prepared alloy, and contact with it is necessary. The tip of the finger is sufficient. We prefer the left thumb, as the experimenter is then more readily identified from the impression by the Bertillon method. Touching the bar in the space uncovered, the triangles are actuated and indicate according to the accepted interpretation of mystic symbols the attitude of the experimenter—whether, in short, he is making for righteousness or the reverse. The bar moves sideways when the contact ceases. A fresh space is thus presented for use by the next comer, and the second impression passes under the crystal coverings where the sun's rays and special apparatus imprint it indelibly upon the bar. That is not all. The position assumed by the pentagram is skiagraphed upon the other side of the bar exactly under the thumb impress, and thus, as long as the four-inch bar endures, there is an exact record of that soul's yearning—at a particular time. You will understand we have only to make the movement of the pentagram in the right direction start an ordinary electric device which frees the bolts locking the door. It was a terrible responsibility giving open access to the hall; by interposing this mechanism we frustrate suicidal mania in the temporary insane. As yet there have been no deaths in the lethal hall."

"And no impressions on the record-bar?"

"That is a secret. Many of us have tried the instrument not connected with the hall; in fact now it is the 'pass examination' for admission to the Esoteric Section of the Institute. We want more experimenters, and if any like to try now they have but to touch the bar before the instrument in the alcove."

"I should *so* like to see the machine work," said the Princess.

"Then your Highness has but to touch the bar."

"But you have the record for ever," she objected, shivering.

"Then touch the smaller machine on the right; it has no self-registering apparatus—is a sort of automatic father confessor. No one will follow your Highness, and none but yourself will know. Although you may not understand the symbols, I am sure you will rightly interpret the indication given by the pentagram, whatever movement it may make."

"I did not mean that I wished to make the experiment," said the Princess.

"Who, then, will volunteer? Fersten?"

That worthy bowed, but thought the first place the right of the ladies.

"Well, any one?" asked Sterry, amused.

Hawkins, prompted by a vigorous nudge from his wife, expressed his readiness. He went into the alcove, followed by Prince, Princess, Countess, and priest. Fersten tried to peep over the shoulder of the operator; the Isocrats remained outside.

"There! It is moving! How wonderful!" said the Princess.

Soon Hawkins emerged, mopping his forehead energetically. The others, having satisfied themselves that the pentagram was stationary again, followed, and began excitedly to talk of the direction a certain point of the star had taken. Sterry prayed them to respect the privacy of the "confessional."

"Let them say what they like; I do not mind in the least," said Hawkins loudly, believing that he had passed the ideal honourably.

"Your Highness next," said Fersten, seeing the Princess still hesitating before the rail.

"It is what Miss Hamilton would call 'uncanny,'" remarked the Prince, stepping further back.

"The Princess shivered and looked at the priest, then at the machine.

"I dare not," she whispered.

The priest interfered. It was magic: the Church forbade magic; he must remind Her Highness of the teaching of the Church; and saying so much, turned and walked slowly from the hall.

"He calls them 'strange idols.' I am sure he is right," said the Princess, looking anxiously after the priest.

The Princess went towards the door, and Sterry

K

accompanied her, telling of the other instruments in the collection, and pointing out the mistake of the priest in confounding the work of science with the rites of magic; but she listened without attention, and he, addressing the Prince in turn, explained how every force will manifest itself if only a suitable medium is presented for the purpose. Irma was listening eagerly to an explanation of the Kabbalistic symbolism from Hilda Kewney, and as the royal party reached the door Fersten caught a glimpse of a Soudanese negro hurrying along the terrace.

"Does your Highness see what that man has over his arm?" asked Fersten of the Princess.

"No; whatever is it?"

"A pair of ten-dollar pants," he said with a laugh.

"Take me by some other way—quickly."

Sterry led them to the south terrace by a private door, then returned to find Redhead and others of the party. Madeline was still at the door of the hall.

"Is any one in there yet?" he asked.

"Yes—Irma; she is in the alcove."

"What next?" And he would have entered, but Madeline resolutely barred the entrance.

"She wished very much to try; she can do no harm; leave her alone, Bob."

He saw the Meysembourg stepping down from the alcove with a very perplexed serious look upon her usually gleesome face, and then, without waiting for her, he hurried back to the royal guests.

CHAPTER XVII.

A PREDICAMENT.

"A NICE little man—Prince Clovis, cordially welcome in Cristallia; and so I told him at parting," said Redhead warmly. "Even Boyd was won over. What do you think of the royal race now, Boyd?"

"Hu!—— I wish Darwin had studied the 'royal family' variety of man as thoroughly as he did earthworms."

"I should like to know what they think of us," exclaimed Beatrice. ·

"Put the question to the Esoteric Section and devise a machine to find out."

"We shall get to know more easily than that," remarked Boyd, "and sooner than we expect. Their visit has done no good. Quite a score of people—twenty-one, to be exact—stood on the quay to get a look at them before they went. It's demoralising."

"The Princess told me her memories would be of a beautiful valley, handsome buildings, dreadful great engines working silently in the night, people strong as Titans, wise as magicians, and cold-hearted as Nature. We have not impressed her for good," drawled Beatrice dolefully.

"She'll be haunted by the pentagram and a Soudanese black in khaki with a pair of ten-dollar pants over his arm." And Robson chuckled.

"Poor little woman! she is quite under the rule of her father confessor. She would have dearly liked to see that record made by the Meysembourg, but dared not disobey his dictum."

"That bit of daring made the Princess feel very inferior," observed Redhead, screwing up his mouth.

"Heaven bless the Meysembourg! she probably saved the colony," exclaimed Boyd excitedly.

"And as nearly wrecked it on her own account. Poor thing! I wonder what has become of her." And Hilda looked enquiringly at Redhead.

"I am going to Europe, and shall see her," said Madeline; then added, in glad tones: "She has promised to return to Cristallia some day with me."

"Bravo, Madeline!" And Redhead nodded encouragingly.

"What is the matter, Boyd?" asked Madeline.

"Oh, nothing; only why go to England, when Alan is in Germany?"

"I did not say I was going to England; but I shall be away some time, and certainly shall see Alan before I come back. I am going in the interest of the State, and shall perhaps be away a very long time." She saw that some explanation was expected, and added: "I have talked it over with Mr. Sterry, and he agrees it is best I should go now."

"Confound the interests of the Commonwealth!— you are always sacrificing something——"

"No more than others do," interrupted Madeline quietly.

"Would any one else sacrifice half as much? And would any of us sacrifice as much for each other as we do for this bugbear of State independence?"

"More, if needed," answered Madeline confidently; "and you as much as any of us, Boyd."

"But what would the State sacrifice for any one of us?"

"Everything," answered Redhead authoritatively.

All too soon came an occasion to test the Chief Commoner's opinion. The relations of Cristallia with Germany, never easy, hardened sharply after the arrival home of the Prince of Calamine. In Saxony shortness of work among the potters gave the Government cause for great anxiety. In the futile manner of the old world, the manufacturers of glass, porcelain, and earthenware had lowered prices to meet the competition from the superior wares. Ten common delft mugs could be purchased for less than one of Jonesware, but the more costly article outlasted a hundred of the others. The industries were going from bad to worse, and riots were not infrequent.

Alan Winship's men would not, or could not, send the news he wanted, so, taking his own transmitter, he started out himself, anticipating no danger. Wrightson, in Dresden, dropped a word of warning, which he disregarded. Beatrice Tyacke remained so much in the instrument-room she feared others would notice and suspect; but her anxiety for his safety overcame all scruples, and she took all messages sent by him, feeling that as long as he was at work she did not need rest.

The shock came suddenly after a long interval of silence and weary waiting. Two assistants were in the room, in charge of other zones, and Beatrice almost fainted when she received the words "Entrapped: rioters insist upon knowing the secret of Jonesware. Threaten my life. Answer quickly.— ALAN WINSHIP."

The message she sent up to Redhead by an Arab boy, and stood at the instrument expecting yet dreading the indicator to start afresh. Would Redhead call the Council? Would he be satisfied to confer with Iltyd? What if Iltyd refused permission? How long would the rioters wait for an answer? Then she thought of what Winship had advised her privately about Wrightson— "a man to be trusted." Of her own initiative she communicated Alan's danger to Wrightson, and besought him to act at once. But the town of Gaben was far from Dresden; still, there were telegraphs and telephones—Wrightson could and would act. So much he promised. An hour passed, and not a sign from Winship; the needle had not once stirred.

A messenger came with a summons for her to attend the Council. Why were they so slow? She could not tear herself away: her place was there, in communication with him. She nodded to the messenger, and he stayed on as she busied herself in transmitting an unimportant communication for New York. All the time she seemed to see into a darkened room in a German hovel: Alan was there, bound, and a dozen ruffians around him; irons were heating on the hearth, and a ladle of lead was being lifted from the fire.

Then the instrument recommenced.

"Answer quick: they are about to torture.—ALAN WINSHIP."

Again the Arab boy ran along the corridor; he brought back no answer.

She dared not communicate with Alan; she knew not whether he was at the instrument or merely instructing some other operator; those about him would know what was being received. If Alan were free he would have some message for her alone.

"Answer at once. I am being done to death.—ALAN."

She scribbled down the message, and gave the repeat signal. Immediately the message was accurately received a second time.

"Do not understand you.—TRIXIE," she worked on the transmitter, as the Arab boy again sped to the Council room.

"We understand you—send answer," was all that came in reply.

Then the boy came back. The Council room was closed; he could not obtain admission.

"You *must* get in somehow, Ahmed." And away the boy went again.

She waited patiently, believing the Council would act quickly and wisely, and so save Alan; but when darkness came on she realised how long she had been inactive, and in that time her lover perhaps tortured to death. The temptation to send a message to him was strong, but she resisted. If a stranger were operating the Sterrygraph in Gaben, no doubt Alan would be called upon to translate any sign the receiver did not understand: she would have used the jargon of their first lessons but for this.

Then it seemed to her that the Council might not consent to give the information, preferring to sacrifice her lover—and her heart sank. She knew Jones's secret, but she felt that *she* could never betray it. What could she do?

The instrument started again. "Glad to die for the Commonwealth. Love to Trixie.—ALA——"

The signs came so slowly and feebly it seemed that Alan could not possibly have sent them—his style was so rapid and firm. But if he really were dying? Or unseen by his tormentors had he reached the machine? Most likely he had been ordered to send one message, and instead had sent this. He had been discovered in the fraud and rudely stopped, as the unfinished message showed. Perhaps for that message to her they were torturing him now.

She sat down to the instrument and worked her fastest.

CHAPTER XVIII.

THE PRIVILEGE OF THE MINORITY.

IT was Hilda Kewney who told what transpired in the Council Chamber; of how the summons to attend came upon her "like a bolt from the blue," and of her consternation at seeing Redhead glum as death, and Iltyd almost in tears. Hawkins was the next to arrive; then Robson, Kell, and Hanlan came in together. Sterry closely following with Fersten, there was a quorum, and the door was barred. A long silence followed the reading of the messages, and was broken by Iltyd, who placed his secret at the disposition of the Council. Sterry then proposed that the vote should be taken immediately. It was acted upon, Robson and Fersten alone voting for the secret being communicated to the rioters. Thereupon Robson, regardless of precedent, proposed that the vote be rescinded, and the best means taken to ensure the safety of Winship.

A stormy argument followed, and when the proposition was at last allowed to be put only three voted in its favour. Nothing daunted, Robson recommenced, refused to listen to any scheme for revenge upon the rioters, held firmly to his proposition that the utmost the Commonwealth could do to save Winship must be done.

The message boy came to the door, and Fersten proposed that nothing new should be admitted, nor any topic discussed until the matter had been agreed.

THE PRIVILEGE OF THE MINORITY. 137

It was carried without opposition. Redhead declared the meeting to be at an end; Robson refused to budge. Standing with his back to the door and threatening any who left the table, he repeated his arguments. It grew dark. The lights were turned on, and still he talked. Then the Arab boy appeared at the window and threw his missive into the room. Redhead refused to read it; Kell, who had picked it up, did so. Again the vote was taken. The parties were as before, and Robson as unyielding. Fersten said nothing, Kell but little; by sheer obstinacy Robson drove the others to confer among themselves and suggest an alternative scheme.

He refused all; Fersten showed that none were so likely to free Winship as compliance with the demand. Then they declared they must ask Toller what could be done. Robson refused to agree. Fersten reminded them of the previous vote. It was promptly rescinded, and to appease Robson, it was also agreed to ask Madeline.

"I won't have it," yelled Robson; "she would sacrifice herself for Cristallia, and so would Alan. I won't have sacrifice from anybody."

"You oppose everything, Boyd," said Sterry, losing his temper.

"It's the privilege and right of the minority."

They invited him to the table again and tried to effect a compromise, but Robson was so earnest in his argument that human life was more valuable than all—to them and to Cristallia—that Jones declared himself on the side of Robson.

"Of course I agreed with Iltyd," said Hilda, "and so the minority became the majority, and at the next vote we were unanimously agreed to divulge the secret. Jones was deputed to send the message himself, so that the least possible number should be in possession of the secret; and on reaching the private instrument-room he found you, Beatrice, delirious, and declaring that you had saved him."

"And so I did, Hilda," answered Beatrice with a sob.

"Of course you knew the secret, and you——"

"Betrayed it. What am I to do?"

"It's all right now—as it happens."

"But it was wrong."

"Not nearly so wrong as it was of us to oppose Robson. We are all heartily ashamed of ourselves, and you have no need to be so."

CHAPTER XIX.

FORTUNE FAVOURS CRISTALLIA.

A GREAT change came over Iltyd Jones. The knowledge that his secret was in the possession of others fretted him, the fear of losing everything became almost mania.

He knew that the Germans, with their working day of fourteen hours, would undersell, and that in Cristallia he could not meet the competition. For the first time since its introduction Jonesware glutted the market; prices were everywhere falling, and there were no buyers. The stuff would be cheaper soon. Meanwhile big prices were being paid for the recipe the rioters of Gaben had obtained.

Plant was being put down in other countries; England and Belgium were starting factories on a huge scale; in America a wealthy syndicate had been formed, and there was a race to be first in the market. Soon the buildings in Cristallia which had been his delight would be deserted, the great engines still, the ovens cold. Successes had encouraged but not intoxicated Iltyd Jones. This great reverse numbed him; he could think of nothing but his misfortune. He hated the sight of Beatrice Tyacke; the mere mention of her name disgusted him. She was soon to be married to Alan Winship, and he would be glad when she took up her residence in London.

There remained Iltydium and his later invention; but once on the track he believed all would be discovered quickly by the eager competitors, and he could think of nothing new. The laboratories had no longer any attraction for him.

Quite by chance he alighted upon a note made on that memorable day when he had invited Beatrice into his laboratory and she had convinced him of the knowledge of the secret composition. Either he had copied the formulæ wrongly or Beatrice had made a mistake. It was one of no great importance —merely the substitution of one hydro-carbon for another—yet a divergence from his method. He obtained a copy of the message sent to Alan Winship. There was certainly a difference, and he hoped again.

"Did you ever make any Jonesware, Beatie?" he asked anxiously.

"A few things—that plaque and the little mug, and one or two other small things experimentally. They are as tough, if not tougher than yours."

"May I have one?"

"Certainly—all if you wish."

He took two of the articles, and hurried to the laboratory. He determined to smash one. Placed in a press, it crushed quite easily. He dropped the other on the floor, and it smashed like biscuit china. The fragments were as brittle as unannealed glass. He was delighted, but said nothing. The next time he met Beatrice he asked casually how long the things had been made.

"About four months," she answered; and he begged of her all the specimens that remained, and for three weeks could not be induced to leave his laboratory.

He was of secretive temperament, but he could hardly conceal his satisfaction. The Jonesware not made in Cristallia would be very inferior; people would find out in what way soon enough; by their dearly bought experience they would ever after avoid it as a sham. The Germans and others were going to drop heaps of money through their ill-gotten knowledge; he and Cristallia would be gloriously avenged. He conceded to the generally expressed wish of his friends and took a long voyage. They thought he might be happy in Japan; he knew he could be happy anywhere.

There was a period of tranquillity in Cristallia. Fersten was still "floundering in the gum," but seemed somewhat nearer the production of "whalebone substitute." He had a great friend in a newcomer, a man named Amber, who was believed to have invented a flying machine, and at any rate was well supplied with money. His syndicate built a factory on the hillside, and at great expense got a steel cable swung across a wide valley from peak to peak. Trial trips of the machine were made on this cable. They always ended in the aeronaut coming to a stop where the wire sagged, and being ignominiously hauled up the remainder of the "trajet" or, still more ignominiously, wound back to the starting-point. He was a man of boundless optimism, and kept on trying.

Beatrice Tyacke became Mrs. Alan Winship, and remained in London. To take her place in the message department Toller sent out Mavis Weyland. Redhead thought Sterry would be pleased, and asked him if he remembered the girl. Sterry thought he did. Soon afterwards he cleared up his work and announced his intention of passing the winter out at El-Aksa, and managed so that he left before Mavis arrived.

Redhead was very busy with experimental work of his own; he ran over to El-Aksa with Boyd to witness the experimental explosion of a self-acting fort in their new scheme of defences, and took with him a curious-looking litle instrument affixed to a staff. He had it stuck in the ground wherever he went, and was constantly "tinkering" at its mechanism. The experiment was made, and declared to be most successful. Robson was not entirely satisfied; he confided his trouble to Redhead.

"It went off prematurely—five seconds at least before I fired it."

"I know it did," answered Redhead quite cheerfully.

"How could you know? You were tinkering with that clock thing of yours at the moment."

"That is how I knew," answered Redhead enigmatically.

"I must try another."

"Whenever you are ready let me know. I will forestall you."

They tried, and it was Robson's turn to laugh.

"Fire away!" he commanded, but Redhead was powerless.

"What have you been doing?" he asked testily.

"Nothing, I assure you. You must go home and perfect that warstick of yours."

And further experiments convinced Redhead that it was the only thing to be done; as yet he had not discovered how to fire a mine without the aid of connecting wires.

When the news reached them that the Saxon Jonesware was rotten they dared not believe it; an immediate increased demand for their manufactures convinced them. Confirmatory evidence of an unpleasant sort soon followed—the Pieterlanders were aggressive once more.

But the forces from the German colony did not come into direct conflict with their own. The quarrels were with the natives, the "friendlies" of Cristallia in the no-man's land south of the Atlas.

Mahomed Ben Hassa asked aid of Cristallia, but fought well for his own. He had his wrongs, and knew how to avenge them—chasing the Pieterlanders right back to their forts and carrying away his women again. He crossed the territory of Cristallia on his return, and the Pieterlanders followed until fire from one of the forts warned them off.

There was a curt demand from the Governor of

Pieterstadt as to the intention of the Commonwealth. It was met by an ungracious rejoinder. "If the Pieterlanders are not fully aware of the intention, they have only to carry the German flag a little further into our country, and so satisfy themselves."

Things began to assume a serious aspect, and Sterry returned to the Capitol.

He met Mavis, and thought how fresh and beautiful she looked. She blushed at seeing him, and was more bashful than she had been when they first met.

"I was afraid you would never come to Cristallia, Miss Weyland."

"I always meant to come when I was free to do so."

"We are very pleased to have you with us, aren't we, Willie?"

Redhead nodded pleasantly.

"Are you going to winter at El-Aksa, Bob?"

"With things as they are? Impossible!"

"Quite!" rejoined Redhead. And he chuckled.

CHAPTER XX.

THE ESOTERIC SECTION.

THE renewed demand for Jonesware brought Iltyd back from Japan in a hurry. He was now feverish for work, full of great schemes, nervous and excitable, but, as all could see, a stronger man for the scare he had experienced. Madeline Winship too was wintering in the colony, and Cristallia was recovering its old form.

The Pieterlanders were troublesome and irritatingly overbearing; such slight diplomatic relations as had existed between the two colonies were ended, and the foreign Consuls in Cristallia could not patch up the quarrel. The Berbers and Touaregs were not so peaceably inclined as they had been, and the Sultan was understood to be preparing a military expedition to the south with the object of maintaining order among them; but action was slow to follow intention at the Court of Abd-el-Azeez, and an outbreak among the Riff Kabyles necessitated an expedition in a quite opposite direction, and the concentration of the fleet off the north coast.

Amber, the aeronaut, had achieved some success; Fersten had almost deserted the gum factory and thrown his energies into Amber's venture. The "flight" was across the valley of El-Tyh, quite twenty-five miles from Port Cristal, and almost on

THE ESOTERIC SECTION.   145

the frontier. Staying there afforded Fersten opportunities for "sport" he could not enjoy nearer town, but his methods were detested by the natives and led to disastrous reprisals.

At last Amber declared his intention of taking a real aerial flight. From flopping along the wire he had progressed to going across the valley with a slack rope from the cable; then the machine mounted level with the wire itself, and now flew higher, held down to the earth by the very rope and gear by which it had formerly been sustained.

Fersten, who was most enthusiastic, proposed a general holiday and a huge gathering to witness the first voyage; for a reason of their own the Council consented. The factories were to be closed for a week, and a regular encampment held at El-Tyh.

Robson and his staff arranged everything; all the holiday-makers were well accommodated in the wide valley, provisions in plenty were stored in the warehouses and marquees, and whether the machine succeeded or not, there were endless charming excursions to be made into the neighbouring valleys, hills to climb, and the fringe of the Great Desert to explore.

Most of the ships were loaded and cleared; the Moors from the barracks, the black servants, and half the guard went to El-Tyh for camp duty; every one who could get away went east. A hundred men of the White Guard, left in town, were drafted in half-dozens as emergency garrison for the various forts; the quays were unsentinelled; warehouses, factories, villas, Consulates, and Guest House all but empty. Before sunset on the eve of the day of the ascent the last automotor took the laggards in a train of trucks to the camp. The Isocrats alone remained; with a staff of operators for the instrument-rooms and a few servants they occupied the Capitol. Hawkins, who did not belong to the Esoteric Section, represented the Council at the gathering; Fersten,

L

whose absence would have been appreciated, insisted upon remaining in town. He had seen the thing often enough, he said, and was not going to shirk work.

Robson relegated him to the south side, and in the event of any unexpected attack from the tribesmen he was to hurry to the Table Point Fort, which was, Robson stated truly, the most undermanned, but, as he did not say, the men were the pick of his favourite guards and absolutely trustworthy.

"Not that there is the least probability of attack; our scheme of defence is too good, and the natives know it. All the forts are in direct electric communication, and any of the mines can be exploded from the central station at the arsenal. If the men cannot hold a position, they leave the automatic guns firing and fall back to the next line of defence. We do the rest, and I reckon a European army corps could not take Cristallia."

"I'll bet my life they couldn't," said Fersten. "How about your ability to attack them?"

"That'll be all right in time. Kell and I know more things than we care to mention as yet. It is of no use to talk of what you mean to do until by experiment you have assured yourself that you can do it. I'll tell you one thing, Fersten; I won't willingly go against any man who stood up for me as you did in that argument about sacrificing Winship, but if you do not alter your game with the natives beyond El-Tyh you'll have to leave Cristallia, and I warn you that if you fall into the hands of old Mahomed Ben Hassa he will make you wish that you'd never been born."

"I do not care a cent for the whole tribe of Mahmouds."

"You leave his womenfolk and offspring alone for the future, or you'll have to reckon with me!"

Robson turned away angrily and went on to the terrace. The moon was shining over the silent town, and for once the great beam engines in the Iltydium factory were still.

"How quiet everything is, Madeline!"

"Like a city of the dead—I do not like it."

"Sorry that poor old ruffian Snyder has gone. Very sudden, was it not?"

"Horrible!"

"I haven't seen Page's report, but I expect it is in. He would have sent for me had it been cholera or anything of that kind."

"Do not talk of it. This fearful stillness and quiet is very oppressive. Do not you feel it?"

"Feel what?"

"I don't know. I have a presentiment that something horrible is going to happen. There!" And she shivered. "That's it again! We used to say it was some one walking over our graves."

"What rot! Why don't you make up your mind to be cremated? I don't think there are three score of us on this side the river, and if the instrument won't work to-night it never will. Shall we get along to the Temple?"

The Esoteric Section met in a small vaulted chamber adjoining the Hall of Science; there were stall chairs in different positions around a star-shaped table, and one end of the chamber had the usual alabaster-lined blind oriel of a mosque; on a daïs within this alcove was a large compass card with an agate-pointed pivot in its centre.

Redhead, Sterry, and Hilda Kewney were already seated when Robson arrived with Madeline; Jones, Kell, and Hanlan soon followed, and the door was closed and barred.

Madeline placed in the centre of the table a four-inch cube of bright metal, on the top of which were cryptographic signs deeply inchiselled.

"I present to the gathering the psychic record of Mavis Weyland, taken in my presence under the usual conditions. You will need no explanation from me as to the value of the indications registered. Their interpretation presents but one difficulty—the inferences to be made from the great exaltation of Hod. We have no record approaching this one in degree; for its intensity, if for no other peculiarity, this register merits careful study." Then Madeline's tone changed from the clear, cold, incisive conventional delivery of the expert lecturer to the guttural of warm enthusiasm. "In Mavis Weyland we have a pure soul, a sincere nature whose dominant note is affection. I move that at the next meeting she be formally welcomed to participate in our work."

Robson scrutinised the cube critically in silence, and looked at Kell, who nodded. Sterry was the first to speak.

"I present the gathering with the last record, taken at 8 p.m. yesterday, of John Snyder, and it completes the series—three hundred and forty-one in all. As you know, Snyder came here a mean, lying scoundrel, determined to wreck the State. Our treatment of him was merited by his rascality. He was absolutely without creative genius, but the work we latterly entrusted to him proved his usefulness, and the frequent records we obtained show that the man not only had his good points, but was approaching that standard of righteousness we respect. For some time past, as the records indicate, there had been a falling away from the level he had attained; he seemed to be under malign influences, caused much anxiety, and excited not a little suspicion. This last record shows that he not only recovered from the temporary lapse from that path of progress we regard as honourable and virtuous, but even surpassed his best records."

Redhead next spoke.

"I have to inform the gathering that the cause of the death of Snyder is certified as narcotic poisoning. The circumstances demand full investigation, and will receive it. It seems not unlikely that we shall

THE ESOTERIC SECTION. 149

discover some details which will enable us to verify our inferences from his 'records.' We may conjecture that he was premeditating some wrongful act, and at the last moment preferred suicide to a worse crime; or, he may have been engaged with others, and his soul revolting, he seceded and was murdered by his associates. It is the most serious event which has occurred in Cristallia, but now and here it cannot be discussed advantageously."

The Chief Commoner's announcement was received in silence, but the impression it made was so grave that nearly ten minutes elapsed before Sterry rose to continue the business of the meeting.

"The experiment we are about to make is to determine whether beryllium, which we know as the 'psychic loadstone,' is capable of being acted upon by an aggregation of individuals at a great distance, in the same way as the near presence of one human organism affects this element. At El-Tyh, which is just twenty-five miles from here, east-by-north, there is at this present moment a crowd of twenty thousand people. In Cristallia there are not five hundred; at Pieterstadt, twenty-five miles distant, about three thousand; and on the large map we will spread on the table you will see the distances accurately marked and the approximate number of the inhabitants of each place written under the name.

"There is, of course, no analogy between beryllium and the magnetic needle; it does not lie in line with north and south or any other current, but is attracted to man—to an infinitesimal extent. To obtain any indication, therefore, in which direction the persons attracting the metal are situate I use a cube of beryllium on the periphery of an accurately balanced vertically pivoted wheel. Earlier tests have enabled me to judge of the size of the cube and the shorter distances at which it is susceptible. This test is to determine whether a concourse of twenty thousand people can affect the metal at so great a distance as twenty-five miles; if it does not, it is my intention to advance in an easterly direction with the instrument until it is affected by the gathering at El-Tyh. We have no counter-attracting influences to north, south, or west.

"The gauge on the broad radial arm indicates the amount of 'pull' in the direction of the attraction; by experiment I hope to deduce from it either the distance or the number of the crowd; perhaps, ultimately, to ascertain both particulars."

The chart was spread upon the table, the company gathered on the north-west side of the compass-dial, then Sterry placed the wheel upon its pivot and set it revolving. When it stopped the indicator pointed south-south-east. Sterry turned it again in the reverse direction, but it stopped in the same spot, and a hasty examination was made of the chart.

"There is nothing in that direction nearer than Johannesburg," said Sterry, perplexed. They tried again and again, with no better result.

Then Sterry entered into details, gave particulars of all previous tests, and they held long discussion of each point that promised a solution of the present failure. At midnight Hilda Kewney withdrew, as she had to take the instrument-room at two o'clock. Jones went out across the terrace with her, and on the way back examined closely the outside of the building. Then he tested the instrument. It was mechanically perfect.

"Give it a good whizz round," said Robson.

Accurately and delicately poised, it spun round for nearly an hour; as its revolutions became very slow they gathered before it and watched.

"It takes longer to go from north-north-east to south-east than all the rest of the circle," said Sterry. "There! see that drag at east-by-north? Time it!"

They did so; there was an absolute retardation when the cube was towards the east; as the pace became slower it seemed as though it must stop with

THE ESOTERIC SECTION. 151

the cube at east-by-north—towards El-Tyh—but the momentum carried it past. It dragged very slowly until it reached the south-east, when it quickened, and reached east-by-north again, stopped the fraction of a second, then dragged on to east-south-east, when it came to rest abruptly.

Reversing the direction of revolution, much the same phenomena resulted, but this time the machine came to rest still further east. Not by any means short of sheer force could it be stayed at the points to the south where it had formerly rested.

"If anything is indicated clearly, it is that a large body of men are moving from the south to the north-east," said Robson, and a great dread came upon him.

He looked at the chart, then at a scrap of paper on which he had recorded the successive directions indicated by the machine and the exact instant of observation.

"Suppose a force starts out from Pieterstadt at sundown, meaning to cut us off from El-Tyh before dawn. They would take the Red Stone Pass. At 11 p.m. they would be about south-south-east from here—that is just where the machine pointed; it is now 4.35, and they ought to be here"; and he put his finger on a spot on the chart. "One-Tree Hill, how does that lie?"

"East-south-east."

"And the machine?"

"Not the quarter of a point out. Look at it," said Kell.

The wheel seemed to be very slowly creeping from south to east; they watched a few minutes, then suddenly it quivered and swung round until the indicator was due south.

"The Germans are upon us! That's another division coming straight for us!" And Boyd gnawed at his nails savagely.

"Nonsense!"

"How else do you account for it?" asked Robson.

"What might be has affected you so strongly you think it must be," said Redhead.

"I'll get out of this anyway—that's a gunshot! Don't you hear it?"

He, Kell, and Hanlan ran to the door. When outside, the sound of cannon-firing was distinctly audible.

"Six miles to the south-east; that must be the Thirty-Camel Fort," said Kell.

"It'll be daylight in ten minutes now," said Robson excitedly. "Jake, you get over to the south side and look after the harbour forts; you'll find the Chief's special motor below the terrace. Take it. Look after the harbour, Morven, and take Jones to put the firing wires round his factories. For Heaven's sake, be quick!"

He went back into the hall and gave the news; told Sterry to start the signal for all to get to their posts, make sure the instrument staff were on duty in the vault, then hurry up into the dome over the Capitol, whither he led the way.

CHAPTER XXI.

IN THE CONNING-TOWER.

THE dome of the Capitol was a camera lucida commanding extensive views to the south and seawards and to the north and east as far as the old line of defences. A number of wires led to the instrument-rooms below, and most of the mines, inland and submarine, were directly connected with machines arranged round the wall, immediately beneath the fine polished mirrors upon which the external lenses focussed the landscape within their range.

Robert Sterry at once stationed himself before the mirror commanding the south and opened the shutter. Two compact masses of troops were shown advancing towards Cristallia and well within range of the guns in the furthest fort; but those were silent. Moving the lens westward, a battery of the enemy's field artillery was revealed upon a hill within the outer line of defence, and it was being well served and directing a brisk fire towards the southernmost harbour fort, where Hanlan's company were replying somewhat ineffectively. Leaving the mirror to Redhead and Madeline, he rushed across the room for a view of the eastern prospect. This disclosed indications of the enemy's occupation of the neighbouring heights. Cristallia was already cut off from El-Tyh, and their own forts in that direction were also silent. A message sent to the nearest brought no answer, and the opposing infantry were to be seen already skirmishing on the Cristallia slope of the hill. To the north nothing unusual was apparent, but from the south-west a small fleet was rapidly approaching.

Robson had been energetically signalling the instrument towers, but from seven only of the twenty-six was the call answered—more than two-thirds of their forts were already deserted or in the hands of the enemy.

"Treachery, treachery everywhere!" hissed Robson.

"The game is up before the fighting begins, Willie. Shall we strike the flag?" asked Sterry despairingly.

"Never! Let us die fighting. What do you say, Boyd?"

"We will give some of them more than enough before we go. But look there! Do you see those pickelhaubers trekking for the Sparrow Hill fort? That is made over to them, I warrant, and they'll turn our own guns on us in less than an hour. Shall I blow it up?"

"Yes," answered Redhead firmly.

"Watch, then!" He moved a key on the switchboard, and depressed a lever. "How's that?"

For an instant there was absolute silence within the dome, but the roar of the artillery could be heard from without; all looked anxiously into the mirror whereon the Hill fort was reflected, with the lines of infantry advancing towards it from the south-east.

"Nothing?"

"Nothing! The communication has been cut!"

"Blazes! We can't hold the town twenty minutes if they get in there! It'll take Morven and Iltyd an hour to close the factories. I'll go over to the old watch-tower and try if that line is intact. You tell all those seven chaps"—(and he swept his hand across the indicator that showed which forts had answered the signal)—"to fire on the Sparrow Hill if they can, and if their fire does not keep the enemy out, evacuate and fall back on the harbour forts. Hurry up Morven, and get him to clear out our whole gang from this side. Quick! Good-bye all!"

Before any could stay him he was gone; the lift chains were clinking over the pulleys, and Madeline was carrying out his instructions to those in command of the forts.

"We will send the news staff over to the other shore at once. Let them seek the protection of the Swiss Consul. Who's in charge, Willie?"

"Kewney, I think. I instructed her an hour ago to advise all agencies to communicate directly with London. What does that mean, Bob?" There was a tremor in his voice as he pointed out the tricolour of the German flag flying over the Table Point fort, close to the town.

"That treachery is Fersten's doing! Great Heavens! The guns there command the road Robson must take. If the devils dare to fire on him, I will blow up the fort! What is the matter, Madeline?"

The girl was white and trembling.

"No, no; you will not kill the innocent with the guilty! Spence, and Brady, and others are there still; they have been surprised and overpowered, and until the wires have been found and cut that German will keep them there to save himself. There is another way! Leave it to me, Bob."

"The wire *has* been cut! See! see!" And Willie Redhead swung his chair round.

"Then it's all up, Willie. The fleet will be within gun range in less than twenty minutes. We shall get it hot here. Has Madeline gone?"

"I suppose so, but——"

"Watch Boyd! WATCH BOYD!"

The fort on the Sparrow Hill occupied a small detached eminence on the sandy plain to the southeast. The defences supporting this outpost were the fort on Table Point, the old watch-tower further east, and the southernmost harbour fort on the west. Robson had crossed the bridge, and was galloping on his chestnut Arab towards the old tower, too intent on his object to notice the changed flag on Table Point. Troops of the enemy's cavalry, followed by large masses of infantry and some machine guns, were advancing steadily from the south-east towards the Sparrow Hill, and for the present were screened from the gunfire directed at them from the harbour fort.

Robson reached the deserted old watch-tower and disappeared within its walls; Sterry and Redhead watching, waited breathlessly, for the enemy were now close upon the Sparrow Hill. To the dismay of Sterry, Robson came out of the tower and led his horse away. When next they saw him he was mounted and galloping towards the fort itself. As soon as he reached the open plain the reports of rifle shots from Table Point could be heard: he turned his head, reined in his steed, and for a moment hesitated, then started forward again. A volley was fired, but he escaped.

Sterry, unable to endure longer, made the connection and sent the spark which was to fire the mine under Table Point, but the attempt failed. As Madeline thought, the communications had been cut. He sent a message to Hanlan, ordering him to fire upon Table Point and blow it up if he could. The order was acknowledged, and then Sterry saw that the German flag over Table Point had been lowered; but that of Cristallia was not run up on the signal mast in its place. The firing at Robson ceased; he had reached a ditch, and dismounting, crept along it, a large case under his arm. After a time he stopped. They could see him delving in the loose sand with his hands.

"He knows where every wire is; if he finds the line in time, the Sparrow fort will disappear." And again there was silence in the conning-tower.

The advance guard of the enemy now occupied the fort; the guns were being moved, and the cavalry and infantry were so close up nothing could be seen of them from the conning-tower.

The minutes seemed like hours. At last one of the great guns in the Sparrow Hill fort fired a shot towards the harbour. It passed right over the coast defences and fell in the sea. Before another shot could be fired the hill rose as though forced out of the ground by a volcano, parted asunder, and threw high into the air great masses of sand, rock, and masonry. There was a terrific crash; houses fell in the town, and even the conning-tower on the Capitol shook, and Redhead cried out with pain.

When next Sterry looked the cloud of dense smoke was lifting from rough hillocks and a deep chasm: forms there were struggling in the last line of the enemy's infantry, now in full retreat. It was Hanlan's opportunity. His eleven-barrelled Gatling guns, with positive feed, poured a stream of bullets into the retreating mass at the rate of fifteen hundred shots a minute, and was silenced only by the first shell from seaward, for the fleet had now reached within gunshot.

"There! That is the way every fort should have gone! It would have needed an army corps to take us then. If only we had not needed wires, Willie!'

Redhead bit his lip.

"We remember what to do when too late. We have the worst of the fight, Bob, but—— Is there any one in the instrument-room?"

"All went some time ago, but there is sure to be one left in the private room."

"Then I'll go. I can do nothing here, and the smash-up is agonising. I'll try to get through to New York before the end comes."

"I'll stay here as long as I can. I shall have to join you downstairs soon. Tell Hilda to save herself. I'll see to you."

Willie Redhead ran his chair on to the lift and

went down. Sterry rushed from mirror to mirror until he saw Robson walking on foot towards the hills on the east and ascend to a hidden ledge where one of the smaller machine-guns was screened and kept always in readiness against possible attack from the wild tribes of the Atlas.

For a time the fighting was seaward. Hanlan had succeeded in hitting the largest of the cruisers, but the heavy fire from the ironclads made the coast forts almost untenable.

As Sterry went round again towards the east he was sickened by the sight of the German tricolour flying from almost every pole on the south side. The enemy had also opened fire from their mountain battery upon the north fort, and a squadron of their infantry were defiling down the hill-road against the arsenal and fortified factories.

Just as Sterry received the message from Kell that he and Jones had completed their work, the sharp rattle of musketry fire was heard on the east. Robson, single-handed, was working the old Gatling gun and mowing down the long file of invaders on the hill-road. They at once retreated, and he, his store of ammunition gone, was creeping from rock to rock on his way back to the arsenal. Then came a terrific crash: a huge shell from the fleet pierced the dome and burst in the quadrangle of the Capitol below, and, as the roof was carried away, Sterry fell to the floor.

CHAPTER XXII.

RETALIATION.

WHEN Redhead ran his wheel-chair from the lift along the corridor to his private workroom he stayed for a minute before a window commanding a view of the south town and forts. The Helvetian Cross was flying from the staff over the Guest House and a crowd thronged the entrance. Smaller knots of people were gathered before the doors of the Consulates, and were being recruited from a stream of fugitives hurrying along the quay. A steamer flying the Norwegian flag had been struck, and was fast settling down in the inner harbour, those on board escaping in boats, barges, and by extemporised rafts. Sailors were also leaving the other ships, and shell after shell dropped into the harbour. At the southernmost fort the fire was slackening, and Redhead saw here and there a man escaping towards the fortifications opposite Cristal Point. Now and again a shot from some one or other of the hidden guns on the north side fell in the sea short of the fleet; but practically the resistance had ceased.

Beyond the south town isolated houses and factories were in ruins, some were ablaze; trees had been sundered by the shot, the cultivated land reploughed and devastated by the continuous wild showering of great shells; the whole place was practically destroyed, and the sight maddened Redhead.

As he hurried along again he forgot all in his fury to assault the victors; any consideration for the cause of humanity or the rules of the great game of war he cast to the winds. Was not Cristallia, the beautiful, being extirpated? He longed only for a chance to hit below the belt, and his intense resentment quickened his brain. He had it! A smile of contentment flitted across his face. In a very few minutes he knew he would have wrought irreparable injury to Germany—but too late, perhaps, to save even what remained of Cristallia.

He went through his suite of apartments, pausing only to take a Sterrygraphic Gazetteer from his desk, and entered a secret laboratory—a private museum of the inventions that had failed, a repository for machines lacking the finishing touch of a genius to make them workable. The room was large and lofty, lighted by five great windows opening upon the northern quadrangle of the Capitol. They were commanded only by the stained-glass lancet windows of the lethal hall, which, to make the room still more secure from the prying eyes of spies, were glazed with fine corrugated sheets, opaque to the outside though transparent from within.

He removed a panel from a tall pillar-like machine and inserted some metallic plates taken from one of the shelves, connected different wires, then closed all up again. He called to the private instrument-room, and the signal was answered.

"Call to London, Cairo, and St. Petersburg; instruct them to signal Spandau, index number G 7408, and repeat until answered."

Then he wheeled his chair to the desk at the opposite end of the room and began to write. A few seconds later came the crash of the shell through the dome of the Capitol. The huge projectile burst as it was falling into the quadrangle. Pieces of it smashed through the windows and wrecked the closed cases in the room; one fragment struck Willie

Redhead's knee and shattered it. He creid out in anguish, but none heard. The ringing of the signal bell from the instrument-room recalled him to the work unfinished. The requisite communications were made now, and if only he could reach the grim pillar-like transmitter at the other end of the room and move the switch-key the experiment would be completed. His head swam, he felt faint, tried to move his chair and failed. He seized a hand telephone on the desk and called to the instrument-room.

"Come here now! Room seventy-seven!"

He tied his handkerchief tightly round his thigh, seized a ruler, and putting one end between the bandage and his leg, turned and turned until he had stayed the flow of blood and numbed the limb. The end of the improvised lever he held close to his side with his left hand, and with his right hand continued his hurried scrawl. Perhaps *she* would not notice; it seemed an hour ere she entered.

"What, Mavis! I thought Hilda was——"

"She has gone with the others; it was my turn." The girl was trembling, and at each more than usually loud boom of the artillery jumped convulsively.

"All right. Will you move that switch-key for me, then stand away at once." He pointed to the instrument he had prepared.

The girl unhesitatingly advanced, moved the key, and stepped aside. The machine vibrated sharply for a few seconds, then as suddenly was still.

"Excellent! I am revenged!"

His head sank upon his breast and his body dropped forward. The girl, frightened, turned a few steps towards him, then stopped suddenly.

"What have I done? What have I done? Speak! speak!"

Her voice roused him. "Nothing; it is nothing. Do not come here. Move the switch-key back, and —oh! oh!"

M

"What is the matter? You are hurt. Let me——"

He put up his hand to forbid her advance.

"No, no; I am beside myself. This infernal din! Can you hear me? Get back to the instrument-room if you can and call to Moscow, Bordeaux, and Stockholm; instruct them to signal Rastatt, index number G 9312, and repeat signal until answered. Then you come here and move that switch-key again. But be quick! We have not much time. I can hear the rifle bullets striking the other side of the building already. Tell New York and London that Cristallia has gone, and that Spandau——"

The report of a shell crashing against the walls and bursting quite near them drowned his voice. She looked up when the noise of falling walls had subsided. The room was filled with fine dust and the terrible stench of exploded picric acid; she could scarce see him, and went closer.

He stretched forth his arm to thrust her away. "Come, be brave. Get to work."

"There is a message from Fez. The Sultan has ordered the ships here."

"Too late! too late! Do as I tell you! Quick! It is our only chance."

His pale face scared her, and there was the odour of something she knew—sickening, fetid, distinct from the stench in the gas-poisoned air.

She put her hand to her forehead and bent forward. "It is blood—blood!" she said.

"Nonsense! You are mistaken. Picric acid, or some vile explosive. Go!"

Then came a deafening roar. The walls shook, there was the crash of falling glass, and then later dull thuds of falling walls and loud shrieks from far away.

"Hanlan has blown up the south fort—that's all. It won't hurt us. Get to work, Mavis; it is our last chance. Tell New York and London that Cristallia has fallen, and the arsenal at Spandau is wrecked by a great explosion. Go! Go! Go!"

His face was livid, but he spoke firmly and collectedly. Doubting whether he was in truth hurt, and believing she could soon get back, she hastened away to the instrument-room.

Rifle bullets, fired from Table Point and the heights above the arsenal to the east, were falling like rain upon the walls of the Capitol. They smashed the ornamental tiles and splintered the concrete walls; some came through the window-casements and the roof; one whizzed just in front of her as she hurried along the corridor, but in the instrument-room nothing as yet was touched, and she went about her work unfalteringly.

No sooner had she left him than Redhead re-commenced his writing, and continued until the loud clang of the Iltydium gong arrested him. It was the well-known signal of warning, and meant now that whoever could must save himself. Notwithstanding the din of musketry fire and roar of artillery, the piercing notes of the shrill gong vibrated clear and unmistakable. In quick half-second beats the signal made itself heard all over the harbour; reached the south shore and the distant forts, and was heeded even by the enemy, for there was a momentary lull in their firing; but, as the mechanically-fed guns of Cristallia continued a steady fire from the hidden places on the hills, the shelling of the town began afresh.

Willie Redhead, resolute to the last, now loosed the lever of the improvised tourniquet, and putting both hands to his chair, wheeled it into and along the corridor. It was a short journey; the goal was soon reached. He touched a press-button on the wall, and the private entrance to the lethal hall slowly opened. With a final effort he urged his chair across the threshold, and then the doors mechanically swung to with a silent snap upon the first victim.

CHAPTER XXIII.

DEATH.

WHEN Robert Sterry recovered consciousness the walls of the dome were pierced in so many places by the rifle bullets of the invaders that he doubted whether he would be able to escape to the lower storeys. Chance favoured him, and although the upper galleries were unsafe, he stayed there long enough to see the ships sunk in the inner harbour and witness Robson's single-handed attempt to defend the arsenal by using the automatic machine-guns. But the enemy were now too wary to advance in close order; on the east their skirmishers were already within a few hundred yards of the arsenal ramparts, and were creeping nearer and nearer the town.

The warships were standing out towards the entrance of the harbour, and had landed troops far away to the south. Then Sterry saw the signals made by Kell to those on the other side; soon the harbour fort was evacuated, then Hanlan blew up the south fort to prevent it falling into the hands of the party marching against it from the coast. Further resistance seemed useless. Sterry determined to find Redhead and see whether he could not now be prevailed upon to order a surrender; for the first time he noticed the gaseous bubbles bursting forth on the surface of the sea in the outer harbour. Soon the water would be a mass of flame, and retreat in that direction as impossible as escape in any other now was. He could but give the warning signal at once, and leave every one to do the best he could to save his own life.

He reached his own office and gave the alarm; snatched up a few papers, and ran along the corridor to Redhead's room, expecting to find him there. He saw where the wheels of the chair left an imprint of dust picked up in the conning-tower, and followed the tracks.

Workroom No. 77 told its own story: the broken glass, shattered furniture, disordered desk, and the pool of blood beneath it. It was easy enough to trace the wheel-marks of the Chief Commoner's chair, and Sterry started in pursuit.

He never for a moment expected that he would be led to the lethal hall until he turned into the corridor that communicated with the private entrance Willie Redhead had himself designed, and insisted upon having. There Sterry thought he saw the "doors of death" closing upon his friend. Rushing along the corridor, he reached the portal to find that the panels were in truth still slightly oscillating. He pressed the button; the doors slowly opened and disclosed the chair standing but a few yards within the hall, and Sterry, unhesitating, ran to its side and clasped the hand of his friend.

"Ah, Bob!"

"What's the matter, Willie?"

The cripple smiled and pointed to his shattered knee.

"Done for; done for, Bob."

"But—it is not mortal! Why did you come here? I say you shall recover."

"No, no! I have done my work. *You* must not stay here, Bob. Go while there is time."

"I will not leave you, Willie. I have nothing to live for now." He knelt down by the chair and looked at the injured limb.

"You must go! Promise me that you will, or I shall not die happy."

Sterry looked round the hall, wondering why ere this he and Willie were not both insensible. The shattered windows and roof were sufficient explanation; the poison was escaping at a hundred fissures, but yet he could feel its effect—a pleasant exhilaration, a longing for and complete enjoyment of rest.

Willie Redhead sank back in his chair, and his grasp of Robert's hand relaxed.

"Go! Go, Bob! I *will* not die unless you go!"

Then Robert felt weary; a strong impulse came upon him to lie down there, just where he was, upon the floor, and sleep. But he struggled against this; his duty was not done; his friend must be saved. He rose and bent down over the semi-conscious man.

"I will go, and take you. It will not hurt you, Willie!"

"No, there is no pain—no—pain. It is delightful. Tell that! But—the—band—is too loud. Far —too—loud."

The fearful booming of the great guns and the quick rattle of the infantry volleys disturbed even the last life moments of the unconscious, fast-dying man.

Robert Sterry determined to move him to some more peaceful place; he felt the narcotic seizing his senses, and he staggered to the door, dragging the chair backwards behind him.

Then as his trembling hand fumbled for the knob he remembered that the doors of the lethal hall could not be opened from the inside. In Cristallia there were to be no "scenes"! And he, slightly under the influence of the poison, was amused at his inability to get out. It pleased him not to be able to do the thing he wanted. He pushed the chair along the smooth floor, and it rolled slowly across to the far side—he and Willie were not to die together after all! He laughed again, silently—and sank upon the nearest couch.

CHAPTER XXIV.

FLIGHT.

MAVIS WEYLAND was waiting in the instrument-room for the signal from Bordeaux when the alarm sounded. The bullets were pelting against the outside wall; now and again the building seemed shaken to its foundations by some loud explosion, and she was ready to sink into the earth with fright, expecting every moment to lie buried beneath the crumbling masonry. She had cried until she could cry no more, and now, tear-stained and trembling, hurriedly signalled again to Bordeaux to make the required call upon Rastatt and set her free.

The tinkling of a telephone bell drew her from the work. Robson was in the Ridge call-box asking for Sterry.

"He is in the conning-tower."

"H'm; where's Redhead?"

The conning-tower had fallen, as Robson had seen, but of this he said nothing.

"Room 77. I am going to him as soon as I get O.K. from Bordeaux."

"Better not wait for that. Go to him, and stay there until I come. Kell ought to be in No. 38. Call him, if you can."

She obeyed, and Kell answered by asking for instructions.

"Yes, he's there. Jones is with him. What are they to do?"

"We must all get out of this. There is one of the small 'crabs' in the north lake; we will try and get away to the 'Gleam.' Tell them to—— Damn! Curse you, you verfluchte churls!"

"What?"

"They've shot me through the arm. You get to the north side of the block as soon as you can—you'll be safer there. Switch all Eagle Peak wires on to the North Lake station before you go. Don't forget! Damn! Damn! That's another!"

"Bordeaux is O.K. I'm going now."

She went out through a private corridor into the quadrangle, now devastated by the exploded shell, ran along under the arched roof of the deserted and ghostly colonnade, and up a little-used flight of stairs to the state gallery. The echo of her footsteps along the empty corridors, glimpses of the unoccupied rooms through half opened doors, or fissures caused by the shot, added to her terror. In the great building there seemed to be no other living being than herself. She had escaped the greater risks of the south gallery, exposed as it was to the rifle fire of the invaders, but was more unnerved by the loneliness than she had been by the threatening bullets. She was glad when she reached No. 77, and called out to Willie Redhead. Receiving no answer, she thought he had gone to one or other of the private rooms, and went in and straight up to the grim, mysterious instrument, of whose nature she was entirely ignorant.

She knew what would follow when she moved the switch-key—that the solid-looking, pump-like pillar would vibrate, bend, throb, and groan like a tortured human being. She felt afraid. What if she could not release the key in time? There seemed force enough within to kill a hundred people. When she put forth her hand she dared not grip the handle. Still it had to be done, and she looked about for something with which to do it.

On the table, near the desk, were Redhead's lazy-tongs, light, strong, and of non-conductive alloy. In an instant she had gripped the lever with them, moved the key, and released it. In a few seconds the machine shook violently, and bobbed up and down as though it were about to leave the level of the floor for an extensive flight. Then it became still. She knew not whether she ought to disconnect the current yet, and looked about for Redhead.

She saw the stained floor, and screamed; went nearer the desk and looked closer. Then she knew that Redhead had been wounded; there were ugly red stains on the paper, and—yes—yes, the last scrawled word was "Valete"—his farewell. She clutched at the sheet and scrunched it into her pocket, and turned excitedly. Mavis understood now why he had not allowed her to approach him. The work he counted of more importance than himself; but now the work was done, and he still in need of aid, and there was no one but herself to help him. Following the wheel-tracks from room to room, she passed out into a corridor through which she had never been before, and on until stopped by the private entrance of the lethal hall.

That portal she had not seen, though, like all in Cristallia, she had visited the lethal hall by the public way. At that time she had not been greatly impressed. She simply thought it like the Egyptian Gallery at the Crystal Palace. This door she recognised at once by its horseshoe shape, the mystic figures, the emblem of death, and quaint motto. But she could scarcely realise that Willie Redhead, full of life and vigour, earnest about the work, and emphatic in talk to her but a few minutes before, had willingly entered the hall to die. What could she do? If she waited for Robson to come, it might be too late: if she went in, what would happen?

She pressed the button timorously, using the lazy-tongs, still in her fingers, to make the contact. The sudden opening of the doors startled her, and the draught along the passage seemed to coax her to cross the threshold. But she was timorous, and held back. With her left hand pressing against the door she leaned forward cautiously, peered into the gloom, and sniffed.

In a short time she saw into the dim room, perceived the back of the wheel-chair right across the hall, and recoiled at the thought of a corpse being its occupant. Then she heard a light laugh, and turning her head, saw Sterry lying on a settee to the right.

"Mr. Sterry! Mr. Sterry! Robert! Bob! Bob!" she cried in alarm.

He heard nothing; understood nothing. His lips moved.

"A success—a great success!" he muttered, and laughed again gaily.

It seemed to her that she might save him. He was so near the entrance; it would be but the work of a moment to dart in and drag him out across the threshold—and he was still living. Yet she dared not venture. The place had always been to her one of horror, the mere mention of which caused her to shiver; and now, knowing nothing of the mephitic vapour with which the hall was filled, the slightly sweet but somewhat stifling odour drove her from the door in fright.

In a few seconds she recovered: she was ashamed of herself, of her possibly fatal delay. She was not afraid to die; that dread had never driven her from her work all through the dangers of the day, but her nerves and muscles were almost beyond her control, and obeyed but the blind instinct of self-preservation. Now her fear was that she, by her blundering, would not be able to save the life of the man she loved, not because she dared not sacrifice her life in the attempt. Her will was good—she lacked only knowledge. The slightest mistake would mean absolute failure. All this flashed through her mind in less time than it took to close her hand on the lazy-tongs and stretch them out towards Sterry. He was not nine feet from the door.

Her simplicity stood her in stead of knowledge. Believing that one breath of the gas would render her senseless, and that the act she had to do must have no obstacle to its immediate execution when once begun, she first knelt down and securely wedged the two doors open by extending the tongs between them and locking them at that length. She would not have time to open the door again by any chance if the wind blew it to, she thought.

Then she took a long breath of the pure air of the passage, kept close her mouth, and sprang into the room. She gripped Sterry under the armpits, pulled him from the couch, and dragged him along the floor to the corridor. His body drew the tongs away from their position, and the doors shut as he was brought through them.

The effort had almost exhausted her, and seeing him lying there limp, motionless, and insensible caused her tears to flow afresh. She stooped down and raised his head tenderly and called to him. Then she remembered that persons asphyxiated may be revived by following the methods for restoring the apparently drowned. She stretched him out on his back and used his arms to produce artificial respiration. After some minutes the chest heaved slightly unaided, and she redoubled her exertions. So intent was she upon her work that she failed to notice that the artillery fire had practically ceased.

Robson's heavy and hurried tread in the corridor roused her. He saw what she was doing, and understood.

"How long?" he asked abruptly.

"Since the gong sounded almost."

"Then Redhead is past recovery. Come along; it is as much as we shall do to escape."

"But you are wounded—and *he* cannot walk."

"Scratches only—and he must be carried. It will have to be the 'fireman's grip,' for I cannot use one arm much."

He stooped and turned Sterry over, then got under his legs and lifted him.

"Hold on, Mavis! And step out!"

They almost ran along the corridor, went down into the quadrangle and crossed it, got out on the hillside, and descended by a zig-zag path. Soon they were seen by Kell and Jones, and these two ran to meet them, joined hands, and carried Sterry between them down the steep slope to the edge of the great tank.

"They are still firing on the south side. How did you get up?"

"We crept up the conduit. We'll go down the overflow at the west end. There is plenty of water."

"Have they got away from the south side?"

"Half an hour ago, in the ocean crab."

"How many?"

"About a dozen."

"Madeline with them?"

"Yes—at least I saw some one in petticoats."

"And where's Hilda?"

"She went to the south side with the others; they are going to the Swiss Consulate," said Mavis, as Kell could give no answer.

"That's all right, then; go on. I'll overtake you in a minute."

"Kell looked at him in surprise. "Where are you going?"

"To fire Eagle Rock. It was from there they shot me."

"Come along, Boyd. There's no one up there now," shouted Kell.

"I'll blow the place up on the chance of there being only one."

He went into the watch-house, and Mavis in a

whisper told Kell what fate had befallen Redhead, and they went along in silence.

Robson overtook them before they reached the submarine vessel. Sterry was still insensible, but breathing freely. They dashed some water over his face, then placed him in the little craft with his head as close to the fresh air pipe as they could manage to prop him.

"It's oxygen he wants. We must be careful, or he'll go." And Jones hesitated about getting into the cramped space in the crab.

"We've got to get out of this. You look after him. Morven and I will attend to the working of the crab. In you get."

They were very cramped, but as they went over the surface of the lake with the air valves open it was not unendurable. They came to the outlet pipe, and then Kell closed the valves. A minute later they were rushing down the great water pipe into the harbour. The crab floated out into midstream, and was swiftly carried into the roadstead. Above them was a mass of flame, their vessel gliding along in safety just off the bottom of the fairway. A few minutes later they were creeping along the north bar, and from there reached the open sea. They thought themselves past the worst dangers then, and the air becoming foul in the crowded shell, Kell made away from the shore and drove upwards the surface. A disturbance in the water warned him just in time to sink the crab again and slip beneath one of the cruisers. After that Robson's order was to keep closer in shore, and they went on until Jones, whose fingers were never off Sterry's pulse, signalled that fresh air was imperative. They ran along just under the surface, opened the valves, and put up the wind-sails. Kell, believing the fleet far away, lightened the crab until even the conning-dome was above water. A look round convinced him of his mistake. He hurriedly closed the ports, and the crab once more was sunk to the bottom.

"That torpedo boat has been following our wake all the way from the bar; we must slip her. Go for the shore."

The enemy were unmistakably vigilant. The course of the crab was altered, and almost immediately had to make a hurried dive to escape a torpedo, the long silvery cylinder all but touching the dome of the crab and its passage being plainly visible to the fugitives.

"Let us stay where we are," pleaded Mavis, alarmed.

Kell looked at Robson and smiled, but Robson nodded. It was a good idea; the torpedo boat, commanded by its inordinately energetic Teuton, would range far and wide in search of them. So the crab lay at that spot until dusk, coming to the surface occasionally for air. They went north again in the twilight, and ran into the little creek where the "Gleam" was hidden.

The other fugitives were already on board. Jake Hanlan, in a suit of blue dungaree, was doing his utmost to get the neglected machinery to work, and soon Kell was lending a ready hand. The "crabs" they sunk in the creek, coupling one to the other, and soon after midnight the "Gleam" was got under way and silently glided out of the shelter into the open sea. The warships of the enemy were still cruising along the coast; a searchlight from one revealed the "Gleam," and a cruiser then bore down in her direction.

"If only we had that new gun ready, Morven, how we would pepper her!"

"As it is she shall run her engines to pieces. I'll slow down just to encourage her. Where are we going?"

"It's no use asking Sterry—he's quite dazed still.

Go north for a bit while I find Madeline and talk plans over."

But Robson's search was useless; there were threescore people in the "Gleam," but Madeline Winship was not among them, and none of them could give him definite information about her. She had not been in the south fort—Hanlan was sure of that. Hilda Kewney had been mistaken for her there; for Hilda had the opinion that it was undignified for an Isocrat to ask protection of a foreign Consul, and so had gone straightway to the fighting line after she had placed her assistants in the care of the Swiss representative.

The fact of Madeline being left behind determined Robson. He would go ashore at the nearest port and try to rescue her. The "Gleam" was afterwards to make for Falmouth and land the fugitives if allowed. Robson suspected that there was an alliance of the Powers leagued against Cristallia, and he warned Kell to give Gibraltar a wide berth, and not to run too confidently towards the Union Jack.

"Keep some one at the machine—perhaps I shall be able to communicate with you at sea. I sha'n't risk any news of importance to England unless I hear first that you are favourably received."

"That's all right, Boyd. Shall I come with you? Hanlan can take this lot home as well as I can."

"You know the 'Gleam' better than he does; you must stick to her. Practically all that is left of Cristallia is in your charge now. I'll ask Hanlan to come with me if he will. Did you 'belt' your factories all right?"

"Tight! Whoever gets into the Iltydium factory stands no chance of getting out alive. I hope none of Jones's men will try."

"Unlikely, after what I have done."

"What's that?"

"I intend to frighten every one off. I saw the enemy were landing marines from the fleet, and they and the crowd from the hills will meet at the arsenal. I guess they'll find that just about the best place to quarter the garrison of occupation, for the Capitol is too rickety now. I have accordingly arranged that some time to-night the arsenal shall go heavenward."

Kell said nothing, and for a time they sat in silence, tired, cheerless, and sore. Kell felt their misfortunes very little more than upon returning from some wearisome, disappointing, and quite unsuccessful hunting expedition—he sat in the bridgehouse just glum and sleepy. Robson's wounds were paining him, and, far worse, his anxiety for Madeline was eating away his spirit.

From time to time these two comrades turned their heads and looked furtively over the open sea to the south, expecting the explosion of the arsenal at Cristallia. When at length it came they were taken unawares; it seemed as though the earth had opened for an instant while the lightning, pent up from a hundred tropical storms, rushed back to the sky. Sea, sky, the heights inland, and the fleet of ships shone like illuminated crystals; then a dull red glow rested for a moment over the land, and again all became dark ere the loud roar of the upheaval assailed their ears. It was a noise so full, distinct, and deafening that Kell dropped the cigarette he was rolling and started in amazement to his feet, even put his hands to his ears as the multisonous echoes reverberated from earth and sky.

"That is the last!" said Kell emphatically, and to hide his tremor stooped over the engine and rubbed away a few harmless specks of dust.

"It's only the first, Morven," answered Robson, quite unmoved, and now unconcernedly holding out his hand for Kell's tobacco-pouch.

CHAPTER XXV.

THE SOULLESS AVENGER.

BEFORE the sun again rose above the mountains of the Atlas the "Gleam" dropped Boyd Robson and Jake Hanlan at Mogador. Both were eager for more fighting, and confident that if only they could induce Kaid Maclean to advance promptly on Cristallia from El-Aksa they would soon be able to "raise the Germans out of their boots."

Then the "Gleam" put to sea and headed north. All that day Sterry remained in a half dazed condition, able to understand but little of what had happened, and looking to others to supply his immediate wants. Morven Kell was too busy running the half finished engines at top speed to attend to him; moreover he thought as Boyd, that it would be best to throw Sterry and Mavis together whenever possible, and Mavis was unwilling that any but herself should wait on him. Iltyd Jones and Hilda Kewney were full of their own troubles, and fell to accusing and counselling each other alternately. Nothing could be planned for the future; the demoralisation of the community seemed complete even to disintegration.

The ship was driving over the rolling billows of Biscay before Sterry's mind became clear. To those about him the return of memory was more mortifying than his delirium had been; he was prostrated by realising the extent of their losses; so great was the anguish of his despair that he upbraided Mavis cruelly for having saved his life. His dejection affected her more than his wild ravings had done, and she struggled hard to appear still brave, hoping that he again would take heart. He seemed but a sorry leader after the Chief Commoner, and she could but contrast the terse, nervous manner of the wounded and dying Redhead with the inertness of Sterry. She had faith that she could win his spirit back to courage as she had brought back life into his body, and bore with him patiently as only a woman could.

A word here and there, an apt phrase, a still more adroit silence befit each occasion and had their reward. Ere land was sighted Sterry began to talk of schemes for restarting the factories in other lands and ultimately of avenging Cristallia.

"Cristallia avenges herself," said Mavis complacently.

She told him of the great explosion they had witnessed from the "Gleam," and he became interested. Then they spoke of Redhead, and Sterry insisted upon hearing every detail she could remember. He was consoled at the thought of Redhead dying exultant in the belief of having achieved a triumphant victory. It seemed not now in the least incongruous that though they had endeavoured to live like angels, they avenged their losses like fiends. The attack upon them was cruel: its repulse, by any means, justifiable. He wished only that Redhead was not mistaken, that in truth the arsenals at Spandau and Rastatt had been destroyed as he thought they were.

The crumpled bloodstained paper Mavis gave him showed only the results the Redhead "destroyer" had wrought. What the machine was Sterry could only guess, and in some degree imagine from the instruments they had constructed at Plainfield seven years before. Redhead worked in private, as was the privilege of all; and although Sterry and some of the others occasionally helped him, it was not always with full knowledge of the work they were instrumental in completing. Undoubtedly Redhead meant this new engine as a surprise. Sterry did not know that at the last minute only Redhead had arrived at the means of making it operative.

Mavis knew nothing, and it was at the present best that she should not know of what she had been the means of effecting. She could point out the machine she had set to work, could describe its position in the room, but not sufficiently for Sterry to identify it from her words, and he was not now so anxious to know which machine it was. Like the first discovery of the workable Sterrygraph, he was overwhelmed by the possibilities the invention disclosed.

He folded the paper carefully and put it aside; then tried to dismiss the matter from his mind, and talked with Jones of fresh schemes for exploiting Iltydium. All the same he was most anxious to have independent confirmation of what Redhead had written.

At Falmouth they were glutted with communications. First and foremost, in their opinion, was an offer from Norway to afford all facilities for the erection and working of their factories and the protection of their secrets. It was at once unconditionally accepted, and instructions sent for vessels flying the Norwegian flag to be chartered instantly for the removal of the Scandinavian artisans from Cristallia to Bergen. In the House of Commons an attempt to unveil the arrangements existing among the Great Powers as to Cristallia had been foiled for the time being. Turning to their own news-sheet, Sterry found brief announcements of the destruction of Spandau and Rastatt. There was no mention of the great explosion at Cristallia, but still more unobtrusive than the mention of Rastatt was the display of "other explosions." In France, Belgium, Germany, and Austria some two dozen minor accidental explosions had taken place subsequent to the great upheaval at Spandau. They were briefly chronicled and without comment. The one important topic of the day was the rumoured massing of French troops on the northern frontier.

The fugitives left for London by special train and sent the "Gleam" on to Portsmouth. Sterry busied himself for some hours with the clerks Toller had sent to meet him. After attending to numerous details, he fell into a troubled sleep in the saloon. He dreamed he was again at Cristallia and in that private workroom from which Redhead had devastated Spandau arsenal. Redhead was there still, taciturn, eager, and with Sterry watching a pillar-like engine throbbing as some of the earlier models of the Sterry transmitter used to do. This instrument had a huge dial like the face of a grandfather's clock, and a balanced needle indicator like the finger of a barometer. Instead of figures upon the face, a name was engraved upon each one of the twelve divisions. Instead of I, "Spandau" was writ large, for II, "Rastatt," and the others were the names of the places where explosions had occurred, if the newssheet was correct. The indicator went from name to name, and Sterry felt relieved as it completed the circle. But it stayed not longer at Bromberg, which stood for XII, than between the others. It repeated; but the names on the dial had changed. Where "Spandau" had been, "Metz" was now written: Liège, Pola, Brest, Spezia, Tula, Woolwich, Cronstadt—Sterry read another dozen, and slowly the indicator vibrated, then darted suddenly from name to name on its way round the circle.

In horror he looked at Redhead, but that face

THE SOULLESS AVENGER. 181

was sphinxlike; then he stepped up to the machine intending to stop it, but could find no key, handle, or lever with which to control its movements. He was puzzled, then became afraid. "Where was the thing?" At once came the answer, mad, grotesque, but all-satisfying as is the way in dreams.

"The key is dead!" And there was a laugh.

"Dead—dead!" Sterry repeated. Then it was useless to look for a solution, but it would not be impossible to stop the machine. And he looked about for a crowbar with which to smash the fell thing to atoms.

As though divining his intention, Redhead spoke. Sterry seemed to see the well-known confident shake of the head and hear the well-remembered voice ringing out in clear, exultant tones.

"That is immortal!"

He heard again, not from Redhead but all around him, the harsh laughter, and he turned away. He was no longer in the private workroom, but sitting, cold, cramped, and fearful, in some small cellar with transmitters of obsolete patterns and strange instruments of which he knew nothing. There was a great mystery, and he was there in that dark, lonesome hole until he found the solution; and he was trying, trying, trying, always ineffectually, to get the message asking the solution through to Redhead, who was far, very far away in quite another world. And at last there came some movement of the indicating needle, and slowly he spelled out the message, assured that it was the key of the mystery.

"It means the end of all wars."

"This did not seem apropos, and he hastily made the signal for the message to be repeated, as used so often to be the case in the old days of the early experiments with Redhead.

"It means the end of all worlds!" And then again came that harsh mocking laughter; and he awoke to hear the rumble of the wheels under his head, the grating of the brake-blocks on the tyres as the train slowed up.

It was chilly: the cool air of the night found a hundred ways into the draughty, dim-lit saloon, but he was hot to fever.

He moved the shade before the lamp and went to the other end of the carriage, where Mavis was lying under heavy wraps.

"You—you are awake, Mavis?"

"Yes; I cannot sleep. I am thinking—thinking."

He sat down by her and took her hand in his.

"So have I been thinking. What is the matter with you?"

"I remembered only just now that I forgot to switch off that machine when I found Redhead had gone."

"Yes!" he remarked, like one still in a dream.

"Will it matter? Tell me! Do you think it matters?"

"Why should it? Cristallia exists no longer; the Capitol and all in it have long since perished."

"Yes, yes, by the explosion of the arsenal. But—but—you can tell me—you know more about such things than I do—is it possible that *the* machine, now it is covered up with earth, buried in the earth itself—can it go on as it did when Willie told me to switch on the current?"

"Of course not. It——" And he paused.

She placed her hand lightly on his arm and looked up earnestly into his face.

"You know?"

"Of course I know. What a ridiculous idea, Mavis!"

"No; you are not sure. I read it in your eyes." She shivered, then buried her face in her hands and was silent.

He knew that he must reassure her. His manner changed. He coaxed her to tell him the whole of the story, and interrupted with many irrelevant questions. At the finish he gave a number of reasons why nothing of the kind Redhead anticipated could have happened, and pacified her without satisfying himself.

When they neared London he obtained the early morning edition of their news-sheet. He scarcely heeded the huge headlines announcing the entrance of a French army into the Grand Duchy of Luxembourg. To him of greater importance by far was the "stop-press" message that the arsenals at Spezia and Pola had both been destroyed by explosions.

Then until he reached Paddington he could think of nothing but that mysterious instrument in the deserted workroom, immobile and inanimate mostly, but ever and anon pulsating as though endowed with life, and by its action destroying far and wide, friend and foe alike. In truth, Cristallia was avenging herself wildly.

CHAPTER XXVI.

PANIC.

It was early morning when Sterry arrived at Paddington. Alan Winship, looking very haggard and wan, was there to receive the fugitives, but he had no news for them from Cristallia. The Sterrygraph system of communicating was at fault. At present only a limited district (between 47° and 56° N. lat. and 5° and 60° E. long.) was affected; but the area was extending, and most rapidly eastward. Roughly, Central Europe was out of touch with their system, and thus the seat of the now almost inevitable great war was cut off from their head station as completely as though a submarine cable had parted.

Sterry connected this failure with the action of the machine left working in the Capitol at Cristallia: for that mischief there was at present no remedy. He suggested that an attempt should be made to get all communications from the troubled districts sent directly north and south beyond the limits of the magnetic disturbance. To that end Hilda Kewney might be able to assist. Jones he sent away by the morning mail to Ostend en route for Bergen. Mavis he took with him to Toller's house.

There a surprise was in store for him. Harry Toller, the best business man in the community, the most commonsense mortal of them all, they found squatting cross-legged on the floor before a blank wall, repeating theosophical formulæ and rehearsing the aphorisms of the Buddhist Patanjali.

Toller owned that he despaired of resuscitating the Commonwealth, which had been crushed out of existence almost. At best its future could be successful only if restricted to commercial undertakings; then it might, he believed, enjoy just such prosperity as other huge industrial concerns, but as an independent state, the experiment of a higher civilisation, Cristallia had gone beyond recall.

Sterry knew not how much to tell him of all he feared respecting Redhead's destroying engine, but he felt the secret so heavy that at last he unburdened himself of every detail. Then he showed, as confirmation, the last written words of their acknowledged chief.

Toller noticed what Sterry had failed to recognise: the two sheets he had were but the last of a series—the earlier ones were missing; they, doubtless, contained particulars of the secret invention it was Redhead's desire to bequeath to the Commonwealth. They questioned Mavis, but she could tell them little. There were other papers about the desk—so much she remembered— but whether any were written upon she could not say.

Both men at once appreciated the immediate necessity of recovering possession of Cristallia. If the papers existed and got into the hands of a man who knew a little—such a man as Fersten—by study or chance the secret of the construction of the destroyer might be ascertained and utilised by their conquerors.

At present their chief hope was based on the probability of the Capitol being destroyed and the machine and its secret lost for ever; but, from the fact that the explosions continued, they judged that the Capitol had not been destroyed, and that the engine was untouched from the time Mavis left.

To obtain the latest news they called on Winship

at the instrument-room, but the messages from Europe were meagre and disappointing. On the other hand, Washington reported that a rumour was current there that the United States Government intended to interfere and prohibit the cession of Cristallia to Germany. But the Isocrats felt that the case was too desperate for diplomatic remedies to avail.

"We must stop that engine, Toller, or Mavis will die of grief. I don't care a hang for the other mischief. My idea is that if Great Britain were apprised of the risk, the Government would soon agree to force Germany to evacuate our territory— at least for a time. For Mavis' sake we must do something."

"It means telling the secret."

"A part of it only. Let us call on Fitzjoy."

Now, Fitzjoy had been pertinently questioned on the subject of Cristallia the night before, and had received notice of several additional enquiries which would be addressed to him in the House of Commons that day. There were no despatches of importance to hand, and the newspapers were inventing details to substantiate the rumours current. He was forced, therefore, to turn to the news-sheets for information and took up "The Moment," the organ of the Cristallia Company, to find only that the publication of messages relative to the Commonwealth ceased soon after the bombardment commenced. It seemed, therefore, that Cristallia had fallen—but it was only a surmise. Sending out for the latest of the hourly editions of the paper, he read that a cargo motor-craft from the Plate for Port Cristal had run for Laraiche upon hearing heavy firing at sea near the port. Other vessels belonging to or bound for Port Cristal had put into Mogador and Casa Blanca. Five German men-of-war were at Tangiers, but it was understood that if they fired a shot the French army in Luxembourg would cross the Sauer. The British special squadron, which should have arrived at Tangiers, was not even mentioned from Gibraltar, and nowhere reported. The news seemed two days old at least. Something had happened, but what, no one in England knew. Fitzjoy was more anxious than any to learn in advance of the outside public. In the old days it was easy enough to block the cables and stop all unofficial messages, but the Sterrygraph put Governments at a distinct disadvantage. Luckily, legislators were habitually wary; already they guessed enough to produce general official indisposition. He felt that it was greatly to his credit that he still remained hale.

The visit of Toller and Sterry was opportune and welcome, but, for the reputation of his office, he had to appear busy, and his reception was curt to incivility. He banged down the lid of a despatch-box and rustled his papers.

"I can give you only a minute. We are on the verge of a great war. What is it?" he asked in tones of annoyance and despair.

"That is it. We want you to stop that war. We have been driven out of Cristallia and can't do it." And Sterry seated himself comfortably in the easiest chair.

"The deuce!" exclaimed Fitzjoy, with a curl of the lip and the smile one sees on the face of a golfer when his opponent has driven hard into a bunker.

"Somebody must put us back. The United States will do it if you miss the chance."

"Great Britain will not interfere except to keep the mischief from spreading. You must do your own fighting."

"It's not a matter of fighting. You have only to tell the Germans to get, and they'll get. You know why, and so do we. If you don't, the Americans will make them get—and you Britishers too."

"Really, this is most undiplomatic!"

"Yes; it's unofficial talk; the matters of form

you'll receive in due course—through the Swiss for us. To-day the United States Minister will see your chief——"

"Hallamshire? He can't. Hallamshire's indisposed—seriously."

"He'll see your chief and notify you that Cristallia is under the protection of the United States, and that if your Government will not act with his in forcing the Germans to evacuate, then Cristallia will be formally annexed to the United States forthwith. That's unofficial, but it's correct."

"We shall know what to do *then.*"

"Doubtless—but you will not be able to do it."

The quiet, confident manner of the American caused a slight feeling of indecision in the mind of Fitzjoy, and he glanced hurriedly at the homely Toller, whose silent, immobile, and complacent features gave to Sterry's words that satisfying moral support the presence of serious-minded business men lends to the speaker of a deputation. Fitzjoy, who was once used to receiving delegates from public bodies, recognised in that look of Toller's the attitude of *the* public—it was like a composite photograph made up from the nation's most influential representatives, and it annoyed him more than Sterry's veiled threats. He shrugged his shoulders and Frenched his hands impressively.

"I'll not contradict you. Cristallia is on a higher plane, I know, *but we shall do our best.*"

"Cristallia is in other hands—in the power of people not so friendly to Britain as we Isocrats were or are. They have a thing which is too big for them, and they are ruining Europe with it."

"How do you mean?"

"The explosions."

"Explosions? They're not in my department. What about them?" And he rested his head upon his hands resignedly.

"The arsenals at Spezia, Pola, and Kiel; the

forts on the Meuse and Sauer have been blown up by the Germans in Cristallia."

" How ? "

" Through monkeying with a buzz saw they can't understand. We used the earth currents to transmit messages, but we lost control when we were shelled out of Cristallia, and the currents are firing every charge of explosive in each completed circuit ; a mass of explosive substance is like a charged voltaic pile in vacuo———"

" I do not understand technicalities."

" At least you know how susceptible is gunpowder to magnetic influence, and that it explodes spontaneously in a thunderstorm."

" I know absolutely nothing, and if I did I would never admit a thing," he said desperately as he snatched " The Moment " and scanned its columns eagerly. " Explosions are not in my department, I tell you."

" The cycle of explosions has not reached Britain as yet ; but it may commence anywhere, at any time. The only chance for Britain to escape is by getting the Germans out of Cristallia and giving us the control again."

" Control of those engines? Those who invented them deserve hanging. It's against international law to employ them, contrary to the usages of war."

" Possibly ; but if we do not get control right smart there will not be a European war—there'll be something worse. I'll tell you what. In ten days there'll be scarcely a ton of explosives left on this side ; then the Americans will have a walk-over. So you must get us back into Cristallia to save yourselves."

" We have determined on our policy, and you may explode God's earth to asteroids before we will alter a single point." And Fitzjoy brought his hand down heavily.

Toller saw the futility of continuing the discussion

and rose to go just as a clerk entered and placed a message in Fitzjoy's hand.

"Half a minute!" ejaculated the Under Secretary, pleased at the interruption.

The clerk, his features inscrutable, mentioned that there was a second message then being uncoded. Fitzjoy put the message face down on the table, and as the clerk withdrew he asked in a softened manner:

"Let me see, where were we? What is it you want England to do?"

"Help us back into Cristallia by ordering the Germans out of it at once."

He shook his head sadly.

"I'm afraid it cannot be done. You may see the message. It's not official, but it's correct. It reads: 'Tangiers, viâ Eastern Telegraphs, to "Beatitude," London. Delenda est Carthago.—FERSTEN.' You understand the allusion. Cristallia is no more."

"The date?" asked Sterry eagerly.

"Yesterday. I am sorry nothing can be done to assist you: we cannot put you or any one into Cristallia, or out of it, for it does not exist any longer. You wanted the status in quo ante bellum; you must be satisfied with the status in quo ante Cristalliam. Now you must excuse me; I have to hold the war-dogs of Europe in check."

When they re-entered the lobby Sterry told Toller that the message from Fersten must be at least five days old; it was probably sent overland by mounted messengers to Tangiers, and had been written in the first flush of victory, or, at latest, immediately after the explosion of the arsenal, whereas, as later messages had informed them, there had been fighting subsequently outside the port, and, as they knew, the destroyer was still at work.

"I could have told him his missing squadron was at the bottom of the sea," said Sterry mournfully; "but what does it matter—the bottom of the sea is not in his department."

Outside they found Mavis and Winship waiting for them. Alan had in his hand the rival news-sheet of the organ of the associated cable companies, and insisted upon pointing out column upon column recording explosions, small and great, in mid-Europe.

"And we can give them nothing!" lamented the journalist in despair.

"It is as well we cannot, or there would soon be a panic," said Toller as he opened the door of the cab he had called.

They drove back to the head station, and by the time they arrived had determined upon their course of action. Winship was to explain, in the next issue of "The Moment," that their communications had been intercepted by the German occupation of Cristallia, and attribute to that occupation the explosions which were taking place on the Continent. To prevent the area spreading, the use of the instruments was to be discontinued and the issue of "The Moment" suspended until the Isocrats recovered control of Cristallia. The news staff in London was to be immediately disbanded and the premises placed under police protection. Toller was to arrange for certain questions to be put in the House of Commons; and Sterry determined to return with Mavis to Cristallia at once in the "Gleam" and endeavour to obtain an entry to the Capitol.

"If we tell them why, they will surely admit me," pleaded Mavis.

"You would then give them the power to injure others as Germany has been injured? No, no, Mavis; we must think of something better than that—you and I." And Sterry took her hand and drew her towards him.

They advised Kell to be in readiness, arranged for Winship to make his headquarters for communications in a Hampshire village, and took train to Portsmouth.

In the House of Commons Fitzjoy, in answer to

a member favourable to the Commonwealth, said that the trouble in Morocco was a purely local disturbance arising out of the action of a punitive expedition sent from Pieterland to obtain restitution from some of the most lawless of the Sultan's subjects ; the district known as Cristallia was occupied by the Germans until satisfaction should be given, but, as he was informed, there was no "city" there, and, so far as he knew, there was no intention of permanent occupation of the Sultan's territory by any foreign force.

Asked if it were not true that the Commonwealth of Cristallia was recognised as an independent State by various European Powers, he replied that none of the great European Powers had recognised the independence of the so-called Commonwealth, and it was unlikely that they would do so since there was no Commonwealth to recognise.

Another member, who wished to know if the Government of the United States had not recognised Cristallia, and threatened to interfere if the independence of the little State were not protected, was curtly informed by Fitzjoy that he could give notice of the question if he thought the matter of any importance.

But the issue of the special edition of "The Moment" produced a great sensation; outside the House the people were panic-stricken, and within it was the one topic of conversation until the rumour of an explosion at Dover Castle caused a general exodus.

Just as Sterry was about to embark he heard a newsboy shouting : "Fearful explosion at Waltham," and he felt that for their own safety they must reach the open sea at the soonest.

CHAPTER XXVII.

THE "WARSTOCK" IN ACTION.

No sooner had the "Gleam" passed beyond the three-mile limit than, by Sterry's order, the few explosives on board were pitched into the sea. When Kell asked the reason for what seemed a most suicidal act, Sterry told him of the risks all who possessed gunpowder now ran. As they were talking the heavy roll of a distant explosion interrupted their words. An ironclad or one of the storeships had gone to its last home. The explosion was quickly followed by another, and then in rapid succession came the rest of a long series, as fort, magazine, or ship was rent asunder and detonated other charges in the immediate neighbourhood.

Already the "Gleam" was far beyond the influence of the current that fired Portsmouth, but its effects could be read as plainly upon the agitated needle of the message dial as seen in the lit-up sky to the north-east.

Sterry and Mavis, and those others of their little band who knew the cause of these explosions, comprehended that the long tyranny of gunpowder was ending. For upwards of three centuries it had been the instrument by which despots had ruled the destinies of nations, and of all its horrors none surpassed the terror wrought by the fearful tolling of its own death-knell.

The sceptre of the future was the unknown "destroyer" in the deserted chamber of the Capitol in Cristallia; it might become, in the hands of the Isocrats, a dictator of lasting peace to the world. If its secret passed to the people now in possession of the place which held it, the most reckless and warlike dynasty of the continent of Europe would not hesitate to use it to bring the whole world into the slavery of the sternest military despotism. There was very much more at stake than the existence of an industrial commonwealth on an African creek— on the recapture and safeguarding of Redhead's secret the liberty of every nation now depended. And Sterry shuddered as he thought how often in the past the wrong people have blundered into discovering means other persons had sought intelligently; for history, like nature, is prone to repeat its mistakes.

In a few hours at latest the particulars Winship had made public would be known at Berlin. Possibly the policy to be adopted had already been decided upon. Sterry hoped that the troops in occupation of Cristallia would be withdrawn voluntarily at the earliest possible moment. Failing this, that France, Austria, Belgium, Russia, and possibly England would urge upon Germany the necessity for prompt and unconditional withdrawal. On the other hand the news, and the rumours, even the direful results which had followed their victory, might determine the Germans to follow up their seeming advantage at all costs, with a view to absolute mastery of the secret owned by the Isocrats. In the former event Cristallia would be soonest rid of the Germans; in the latter, Germany, absolutely deprived of all available munitions of war for the time being, if not overrun and vanquished by the French, would succumb quickly to the expedition sent across the Atlantic by the United States of America.

Another danger, and a real one, was the possibility of the accidental discovery by the invaders of Redhead's description of his destroyer, and so identifying the machine and its purpose as to experiment with it in connection with the message transmitters. If, as Sterry believed, the Capitol was only a heap of ruins, this danger was not an immediate one. When the German commander at Cristallia was informed of the particulars Sterry had deemed it expedient to make public in "The Moment," no doubt some search would be made to discover the machine; but the "Gleam" would reach Cristallia before any message from Europe could be delivered there.

The next day they overtook several Norwegian steamers bound for Cristallia, and, when it was nearly dark, sighted a German warship to the south, which approached near enough to recognise the "pyramid and diagonal" flying at the masthead of the "Gleam," then went about and raced to the south-west, where she was lost in the darkness.

The "Gleam" was almost abreast of Mogador when Mavis noticed that the message-indicator was vibrating regularly. The call was answered and a communication received from Robson's agent at El-Aksa, to the effect that the invaders were now pent-up in Cristallia. The German fleet had been driven to the south, and the Sultan's ships were in pursuit. Kaid Maclean had outflanked reinforcements from Pieterland, and was pushing them back over the Wady-Dra. Hanlan was keeping a brisk fire on the enemy's earthworks before Cristallia, and Boyd Robson himself was returning from a chase after Fersten and his party of mutineers—now in the Great Desert. The Capitol still stood, the enemy not daring to enter any of the buildings on the north side after the lesson they had learnt from the blowing up of the arsenal. Robson wanted the "Gleam" to cruise about the roadstead and prevent any escape by sea while the Moors endeavoured to drive the invaders north towards the Fort Chanak or on to Agadir.

Kell was afraid to venture close in shore under

Agadir until Sterry reassured him, by explaining that there was no danger to be apprehended from explosions. The currents which fired the stores in Europe passed too quickly through Africa to take effect—just as a charge of fulminate will burn through a train of gunpowder without exploding it. The "destroyer" was set for latitude 50° N, and places more than ten degrees to the north or south of that line were not affected. The ships before Cristallia, therefore, had not been blown up; it was probable that the Germans ran short of ammunition and went south in search of further supplies.

Unobserved from Cristallia, they ran the " Gleam " into the north creek, and found there a Moorish outpost. That very night Robson's force was to act in concert with the troops of Kaid Maclean in a joint attack from south and east upon Cristallia.

Sterry thought he could be of real service within the town if only sufficient men could be smuggled in to defend the approaches to the Capitol until the attack from the outside should commence.

To that end they first took a small quick-firing gun from the deserted fort and put it in the " Gleam," then with all the Moors available they went to sea, taking the smaller " crab " in tow. Before the ship passed round the point into the view of those on the heights above Port Cristal, Kell, Sterry, Mavis, and two of the Moors were lowered into the " crab," and the " Gleam " then returned to the creek for the other submarine boat.

The " crab " was floated along the surface until the roadstead was reached. The town was in ruins and almost deserted; German flags were flying from the remains of the fort and some improvised defences on the north shore. The pinnacle of Iltydium was battered, but still stood erect on its base. The harbour was choked with débris, the shores littered with half-burnt baulks of timber, and on the surface of the water a few patches of smouldering scum

THE "WARSTOCK" IN ACTION.

indicated that the gas reservoirs were even yet not quite exhausted.

To avoid discovery the crab was sunk before entering the harbour, and scarcely emerged a few inches until it touched the north shore, where the conduits by which they had escaped from the Capitol opened into the river from the upper lake. A line of German sentries was posted on the quay, but so far from the ground level was the crab that the four passengers entered the huge pipes unobserved, and the crab, with Kell, slipped back again into deep water.

On foot they crept along the dark slimy drain, seeing nothing, and groping blindly forward and upward. They had proceeded about halfway when the pipes vibrated as though shaken by an earthquake. The terrified Moors hesitated, and would have turned back but for Sterry's command to proceed. At last all emerged safely on the south side of what had been the great north lake—a sheet of water now drained to insignificant puddles and its east end choked with débris from the arsenal. Far away to the west a few German sentinels could be distinguished; on the grass-covered, well-timbered pleasant slopes of the hill ascending from the north shore there was an encampment of the enemy; but the south strand, the terraces, gardens, and buildings all seemed quite deserted.

The Capitol was in ruins: the great dome had disappeared; the tower which had supported it was little more than a framework of girders and pillars, which appeared to be toppling over towards the south. Some of the pillars were badly bent, most were out of the perpendicular, and some of the huge joists drooped at different angles, held up only by one or two bolts. From the building itself most of the tiles had been shaken; there were great gaps in the walls where the concrete and plaster had fallen out; other parts were practically whole. In the still, clear air of the twilight it stood out so plainly that they could scarcely believe their eyes when they saw the whole structure quiver. A few tiles fell from the sides, another block of concrete nogging dropped inward; then, all was still and silent again.

Sterry knew the way well, but went ahead cautiously, pointing out to the Moors the road by which they must conduct the party whom Kell would bring later to reinforce them. There was a complete cordon of sentries around the Capitol, but far distant from the crumbling building, so the conduit gave admission within the line, its existence being probably unknown to the guards

It was not quite dark, but the short twilight was fast waning and the fires in the opposite camp could be seen distinctly when Sterry sent the Moors back, and himself, with Mavis, alone entered the deserted building by a private door in the west wing.

The shattered windows, the plaster-strewn stairs and corridors, the disordered rooms and fallen walls were heartbreaking. Sometimes a room seemed to have escaped the general wreck, and this made the ruin of the others seem worse.

By the least-used passages Sterry led to the first floor; more than once he paused thinking he heard unusual noises, but quickly reassured himself. In that great building it would be strange indeed if there were not many sounds he failed to recognise. Passing quickly along a corridor, they were brought to an immediate standstill by the banging of a door and a sudden shock—like to nothing but the sudden grazing of a fast-driven ship over a sandbank.

The building was shaken to its foundations; the sharp successive jerks almost threw them off their feet; there was a loud whirr like the rattle of ten thousand fast-driven spindles; then the convulsions ceased, but the building still vibrated slightly, so great was the force that had moved it.

THE "WARSTOCK" IN ACTION.

"It's the machine — the machine!" whispered Mavis, and she dragged Sterry forward.

Soon he stopped again. There was most certainly a noise within the building—a faint footfall, like the tread of a person going cautiously on tiptoe. It pattered along some distant passage, then died away.

"Some of the Moors. Quick! before it begins again." And Mavis tugged at his arm.

In a few minutes they reached the Chief's state apartments, and passed through them to Redhead's suite; then, crossing the corridor, entered the private workroom.

Apparently no one had been there since Mavis had left hurriedly in pursuit of Redhead. The machine stood there, and as she stepped towards it the vibrations recommenced, more violent than any she had seen. It shook everything in the room and made the whole building tremble. Without heeding now she would have seized the switch-key there and then with her naked hand, but Sterry's arm barred the way. Not until the machine was quite still would he allow her to touch the key even with the rule he picked up from the floor.

Then the machine once more rendered harmless, they went hand in hand to the desk. Not a paper remained upon it.

"I am sure there were papers here," whispered Mavis.

"They have been shaken down."

Mavis stooped and peered under the tables; then sprang up suddenly, clutched at Sterry's arm and shuddered.

"I'm frightened—I don't know what it is. Don't look! Don't look! Come away!"

"We will get down into the instrument-room then. Take care not to tumble, or some sentry may hear us. Take my arm."

They were about to go out by the door through which she had followed Redhead, but she hung back.

"Not that way!" she whispered.

Sterry nodded. The loneliness of the place was growing upon him too, and they walked along on tiptoe, scarce daring to speak; nervous, apprehensive, easily startled as the conscious-stricken evil-doer. So they passed through two laboratories and approached the study.

Something dark flitted across the half-opened doorway, and Mavis stopped short.

"Did you see that? Listen! Listen!"

But all was still, so still they heard their own hearts beating; then Mavis drew a long breath, and half stepped, half glided to the door of the study and peeped into the room.

Sterry followed so closely that, as she reeled away from what she saw sitting there in Redhead's armchair, he caught her in his arms and placed his hand over her mouth to still her scream.

CHAPTER XXVIII.

"FOIGHTIN' LARRY AV THE GUARD."

"COURAGE! For Heaven's sake, courage, Mavis!"

She was trembling violently, but suppressed her cry, and would have leaned forward again to see into the room, but Sterry restrained her.

"Did you see it?" she whispered.

"The enemy," he breathed in answer. "Listen!" And his hand slipped to his hip pocket.

There were two figures discernible now; one, seated in the wheel-chair, was peering hard at some papers held close before his face; the other, near the corridor door, was listening intently.

"Nothing," he said abruptly in German. "Go on."

"Colossal!" ejaculated the other, between muttered words of English and German.

"Good?" asked his companion, his eyes still on the door.

"Immense! But I cannot see to read more. We have something worth taking at last." And he laughed nervously as he folded the sheets of paper.

"Where will you hide them?" asked the bigger man.

"I wish we could identify the machine now——"

"It is too dark. Where will you hide the papers?"

"I will take them."

"Give one to me then."

The translator gave a folded slip to his companion, who proceeded to fold it more tightly and fumbled with the collar of his tunic, while the other removed his left boot and put the uncovered foot across his knee. So fully were they occupied in secreting the documents that Sterry determined at once to act.

"Help me, Mavis," he whispered. "Close and lock the door when I ring the bell."

He vanished into the passage. A few seconds later, when the translator was struggling with his boot and the young officer was buttoning his tunic, an electric bell rang in the corridor, and almost immediately afterwards a door was flung to with a loud bang, and Sterry in stern tone called: "Halt! Ergeben!"

The Germans had no intention of surrendering; they started for the other door, but Mavis closed it in their faces. As she moved out towards the passage they rushed through the room in which she was and gained the workrooms beyond. Sterry darted along the corridor, hoping to reach up with them, but Mavis flung her arms round him and besought him to stay.

"They will kill you, Bob!"

"They have the secret. Let me go!"

"No, you shall not; they are desperate. What does it matter if they have the papers? they have not got the machine. We can lock that up. Perhaps they will come back for it. Then you can take them."

Sterry, though in despair at the loss of Redhead's papers, could scarcely forbear a laugh at the girl's simplicity. The start the thieves had obtained rendered it hopeless to pursue now, and, if he reached up with them, it was unlikely that he could overcome them. Possibly they were still hiding in the building, and would, as Mavis suggested, return to identify the machine. They made fast all the doors of the private suite; then, as silently as possible, they walked along the corridor and groped their way downstairs by the unused steps near the lethal hall. They were startled by a loud shriek of terror—apparently from some one within the building, and not far from the passage they had just left. Almost immediately it was succeeded by the report of a rifle from without—then again all was still.

"What is that?"

"Perhaps a sentry firing at those runaways. If he has not dropped one they may be driven back. We must be careful; we can hide somewhere if any enter the building to search."

If the German thieves had really come to grief, their end was timely and well merited. Sterry listened, hoping for some further assurance of their end, but the building was full of strange noises he could not identify, and he resumed his way along the corridor to the dark hall under the dome.

It was not easy to find the particular switch-keys they wanted, for they dared not light up the room, and neither knew in what state the operators had left the instruments or the connections. Sterry and Mavis longed for tidings from the refugees on the south side, and could easily enough have communicated with any station there, but the success of the attempt they were about to make depended wholly upon their presence in the Capitol being unknown to the enemy until the fight began.

They could hear the distant firing of the outposts on the east and south. The troops commanded by Robson and Kaid Maclean were already advancing to the attack. Kell seemed long in coming, but at last they heard the uncertain tread of some heavy man slowly approaching by the dark corridor. He came near enough for Sterry to distinguish a fez and the folds of a burnoose, but the footfall was not that of a Moor, and Sterry, revolver in hand, challenged the intruder in Arabic.

"Maloom—maloom," answered the figure, instead of giving the password agreed upon.

"Who are you?"

"Faith, and if it isn't Mester Sterry himself! The Lord be praised, you're alive, sorr!"

"Is it Gibbons?"

"That same, sorr! It is Oi—Larry Gibbons—'Foightin' Larry av the Guard,' sorr!"

And Sterry discerned that the strangely clad figure stood to attention in the strictly military fashion so dear to the dignity of Boyd Robson.

"What has happened?"

"Sure, sorr, and it's myself'd make bould to ax that same question, sorr, seeing as Oi've been made prisoner since before the foightin' was, wuss luck!"

"And you have escaped?"

"'Zackly so, sorr, seein' as how Oi have giv' my parole the slip, so to spake, not bein' able to keep my hands from sthranglin' the varmints when Oi heard the guns a-firin' yonder, sorr. So Oi just shlipped into the wather and paddled over to this soide, and crep' along until Oi found this old clout of Ahmed's at the gatehouse, but divvil a weapon could Oi find at all, at all, so Oi was forced loike to put my fist agen the first haythen 'Yah-yah' Oi seed struttin', bould as an Orangeman on parade, and thin Oi put a shot into him out av his own rifle, sorr! that his mates may think he took his own worthless breath—the which you may have heard, sorr—and Oi came next straight on here to foind some sort of a gun with which to load up their haythen carcases with lead, sorr! Afore the General comes, sorr! Bad 'cess to them, kaping him back, says Oi."

"Where are the other prisoners? Is Miss Winship with them?"

"Lor' bless your soul, no, sorr! The poor swate, innocent darlint's dead, sorr! She is, sorr! Oi seed it done with my own oies, sorr! At the very outset, and the one that did it, sorr, was that never-to-be-forgiven demoralised scoundrel of a blackguardly haythen 'Yah-yah'—may our gracious Lady forgive me for callin' the bloothy murtherer and villain by so honourable a noime, the which Oi would not save för the presence of yer honour's lady, sorr. Fersten's his name, sorr!"

The news froze Sterry; he sat silent and motionless as the Irishman continued, and Mavis, creeping closer and closer to his side, at last rested her head upon his shoulder and sobbed as though her heart were breaking.

"It was loike this, sorr. Oi was sleepin' the swatest slumber in my bunk, when Oi found my arms sazed and half a dozen men atop of me. They swaddled me and the rest of us up tight, and gagged us with our own pouches, but Oi seed 'em, dirthy bone-boilers from the gum factory, and the chap as were a-sittin' of me were a Pieterlander—Oi *smelt* him, sorr! Then, whin it got loight and the foighting began, we was huddled into the cistern, and Oi comprehended what was afoot. The 'Yah-yahs' was a-marchin' into the fort, when in comes the poor dear lady and orders them not to fire on the Gineral —which was their intention, sorr; and spakin' so swate was she they did at last heave down the renegade rag, sorr, but divil a bit durst they run up the flag. Then Fersten roides up a-swearin' and blackguardin', and no sooner claps eyes on the poor dear girl than he outs with his pistol and foires roight atween her oies. She dropped stark dead— poor soul!—within two foot of where Oi was lying; and it 'most killed me, it did indade, sorr! Then the foightin' goes on all day, sorr; and pity they was allowed to live. Oi could tell by their ways how 'twas a-goin', for or agen 'em; and when there was a big 'splosion they nearly dropped with froight, the spalpeens! But it was when the arsenal went up they was hit wust of all, and serve 'em roight too, sorr! 'The Isocracy is a-elevatin' of yez,' sez Oi to myself, 'but you'll never reach their level!' Then for days and days we wuz kept close in prison at the fort over yonder, sorr, and to-day they took our word to return at sundown, and let us out; and Oi slunk off, as Oi've already tould you, sorr, and it's only a weapon Oi wants the now to be happy with 'em—and help the Gineral a bit, sorr! Lord preserve him!"

"Here comes Captain Kell, who'll find you a gun of some sort."

"One of thim hundthred barrel'd uns, plase, sorr, and as many cartridges as ye can spare me."

"How many are there of you, Kell?"

"Twenty-one Moors and Tom Clegg. You'll help by taking one of the Gatlings, and Larry can have another. They've begun firing already away on the east, and I expect they'll send up reinforcements from the arsenal fort, which'll be zeep! They could shell us into smithereens in a twinkle from that side, so the more out against Boyd the better. I put a time detonator on one of the harbour mines, and when that explodes the "Gleam" will open fire on the old harbour fort. We shall follow. Wait until all are out on the open—they're sure to march up reinforcements to the fort along the quay. We won't begin until the first are almost there, and no firing from the north or east sides until the very last. We don't want those on the fort to know where the mischief is coming from, and they can't see the south terrace from there. Gosh! won't they holler!"

"There seems to be more fire in the harbour."

"The outlets were choked up, so we cleared them a bit—there's enough vapour left in the tank to make a fair blaze again to-night, if only it can get out."

"I'll try to make a little diversion for them at the other end of the town—it will be all right if the wires are connected up correctly. You must find plenty for the Irishman to do."

"I'll put him in the thick of it on this side, and rig out one of the automatics as well. Then you

"FOIGHTIN' LARRY AV THE GUARD." 207

three must hold this fort. Clegg and the Moors will keep matters brisk on the other if they attempt to storm this building. Everything depends upon holding this place, where we can give it them hot as they are driven back."

He went away to the north side, and the Moors got the machine-guns out of the guardroom and arranged them on the terrace front. As soon as it was quite dark outside, searchlights were flashing from the fort upon the Capitol, the town, and the plain to the south; from the harbour fort other lights were sweeping the horizon seaward. Over each of the Consulates and the Guest House seven red lamps were hung in the form of a cross, and reinforcements of infantry were crossing the upper bridges to the south side, where the firing of the attacking party was brisk.

Sterry did not see the submarine explosion in the harbour, but it was soon followed by a three-inch shell from the "Gleam" falling in the harbour fort. There was an immediate stir on the south side of the town, and companies eight and ten deep were marching westward along the quay; soon some five hundred men were mustered on the exercising-ground before the barracks. It was hard to keep from firing, but Kell had fixed the automatic gun at one of the open spaces on the south side to cut off communication from the east, and its firing was to be the signal for the commencement of the slaughter, Gibbons, at the other end of the corridor, being instructed to keep clear the quays on both banks. Sterry was to confine his shot to the exercising-ground, the south plain, and any roads to the east he could cover. The main point was to have the enemy mustered in the open in force before firing a shot, then clear all off before any could escape.

For this purpose the companies marching along the quay to reinforce the harbour forts were to be allowed to go to the utmost limit before being shot down, and as the other reinforcements reached the same point they were to suffer the same attack; if successful, half the garrison of occupation would be cleared out before aware of their danger.

Unable to wait longer, Sterry moved the switch, but the communications were disarranged so that instead of blowing up the bridge as he wished, the only immediate result was to light up the dilapidated pinnacle on Cristal Point.

The troops, alarmed, were advancing at a double; in a few seconds those in ambush in the Capitol would open fire, and on the success or failure of that fire would depend whether the enemy would attempt to storm the building or themselves be annihilated.

CHAPTER XXIX.

THE LAST STRUGGLE FOR SUPREMACY.

THE special machine-guns kept for the defence of the Capitol were all fitted with "silencers" which stifled the report of firing, muffling the sharp crack, and producing only a whirr not audible more than fifty paces beyond the guns. When Larry operated his weapon, the companies in close marching order upon the quay suffered badly; the men fell dead in the ranks and there was no indication of the point from which the bullets, that dropped thick as hail, were being fired. In the immediate panic that ensued the survivors of the foremost company turned, collided with those following, and caused a delay in reaching cover by which Larry did his utmost to profit. He paused only when it was necessary to change the exhausted ammunition feed-boxes, and in a few minutes the deadly silent fire had demoralised the whole force on the quay and put every individual at his mercy.

There were still men to be seen in the exercising-ground, and Sterry directed his fire to that point until the ammunition-box was again empty. The reinforcements marched across to Table Point fort were now returning; readjusting his gun, Sterry next opened fire upon them, and maintained it until Kell came to him.

"All quiet on the north side still, and not a soul left standing on one of the quays. Shoot down all you see. I've put in another 'automatic' to keep the river bank this side, and sha'n't come back here until daylight unless driven off."

Sterry obeyed Kell's command implicitly. Not a form appeared in the open within range of his gun but he sent a hundred rounds as near to it as he could aim them.

Practically no response was made to their fire; an attack from within was unexpected, and the troops within range could not save themselves. To the sentries and garrisons of the fort and trenches the dark building of the Capitol seemed still untenanted. From the quays below it showed clearly enough against the skyline, but none aimed at it at the right elevation to reach the ground floor; the upper walls and roof alone suffered from what little fire there was in return.

Sterry was still busy — aligning his gun now at small groups, isolated individuals even — when suddenly shooting commenced on the north side of the building. It lasted but a few minutes, and was followed by much sounding of bugles on the heights above the fort, answering calls from the valley and plain. Then the enemy ceased firing in the direction of the town and Capitol both, but Sterry and the two Moors serving his gun worked the harder.

The telephone call bell rang close by Sterry, and he left the gun-crank an instant to listen to Mavis in the instrument-room. She said that the Swiss Consul wished to know on what terms the invaders might surrender.

"On no terms—they must clear out." And he went back to the gun, for which he had already acquired a liking.

Soon he was again interrupted.

"On what terms a truce for twenty-four hours?"

"No truce—neither for a month nor a minute! Ring them off!" And he recommenced shooting with increased zest. Their fire was telling upon the enemy.

THE LAST STRUGGLE FOR SUPREMACY. 211

"They surrender—they ask for quarter," called Mavis.

"No quarter!" yelled Sterry, as he still turned at the crank of the gun; "we—are—automatic." And he laughed as he saw that the little knot of men which had been gathered behind a transport-waggon was now a confused heap not higher than the wheel-naves.

The garrison of the Table Point fort had been driven out from the south and were in full flight towards Cristallia town across the plain. Sterry got his gun quickly into action upon them. Firing recommenced from the north side, but the search-lights no longer shone out from the fort—those heights had been evacuated and the enemy were in full flight towards the north creek. The advance-guard of Robson's division in pursuit had already reached so near the Capitol as to separate the enemy's forces into two distinct corps acting independently of each other.

Robson was driving the Germans on the north side towards the sea; those of the enemy on the other shore were in even a worse predicament, without shelter, organisation, or leaders; and the firing continued until daybreak, when the pyramid and diagonal flag of Cristallia could be discerned flying side by side with the "red rag" of Morocco over the German Imperial Eagle on the barracks and arsenal fortifications, and white flags flapping here, there, and everywhere about the lower town, from which the German tricolour had disappeared.

Sterry ceased firing and went over to the Irishman's gun, still pumping forth its stream of metal at short intervals. He felt vexed that at this furious game he and the best of the Isocrats were probably no better than the hard-headed, soft-hearted Irish labourer—from the soldier's point of view possibly not so good owing to inferior skill. He told the gunner somewhat savagely to cease firing, and himself went to the automatic self-ranging machine-gun which was aligned upon the cross-ways. In that open space was a Red Cross ambulance waggon riddled with bullets; the mules dead, and an ugly heap of those who had attempted rescues lying about it. For hours it had been the butt of thirty musket shots a minute from the machine—which did not discriminate between fighters and non-combatants.

This reminded him of the instrument in Redhead's room, and he was savage at the thought of its secret being in possession of the enemy. Not one of the invaders should be allowed to leave Cristallia until the papers had been discovered, though the difficulty of discovering the present possessors seemed insurmountable. Already the Germans on the south side were surrendering to the Moors advancing towards Table Point—possibly on the north side the same thing was being done, and the bearers of the papers might get clear.

He found Kell, and hastily arranged what had to be done. Kell thought that the men were still in hiding near the building, for the shot Sterry and Mavis had heard was undoubtedly that of Larry Gibbons in despatching the sentry; the shriek was merely a coincidence, for the sentry had died without so much as a moan. It was imperative that the Germans should not cross the river either way, and the prisoners on the north side, as well as the dead and wounded, be thoroughly searched.

They got their own staff across from the Guest House and started the instrument-room in full force. Then they set the Moors to collect and strip the dead and carry the wounded into the great ferry house on the north quay, Gibbons being placed in charge, with orders to shoot any German crossing from the south side or escaping in that direction. On the plain and in the south town the ambulance corps were very busy, but having no assistance from the Moors or Cristallians.

When at last the pursuing party returned from the north there were other prisoners and a disorderly array of Kaybles and Touaregs under Hanlan. It was arranged to strip these prisoners of war at once in one of the warehouses and fit them out in suits of dungaree, grass sandals, and fezzes from the factory stores, then keep them close prisoners in the motor factory yard.

Robson, still sore from his wounds and hardened by the cruelties of the short campaign, had but one duty to perform before starting out with Kaid Maclean to attack Pieterstadt. "I don't care what becomes of the prisoners. Shoot them, if you like. Better send them overland to Fez; that will be a hard walk for them, and those who outlive it will make a pageant for Abd-el-Azeez. What we have to do is to bury our own dead—then sack Pieterstadt. That's enough for the day."

"What about the dead Germans?" asked Kell.

"Put the bodies in a refuse hopper and tow them out to sea, or there'll be the plague to finish off us survivors. What is to be done with Redhead, Bob? We've shut off the vapour and opened the fans. I'll go in presently."

"Where would you suggest, Boyd? They must be buried together, of course. Then you'll go after Fersten again."

Robson shook his head.

"Fersten's done for by this. We drove him into the clutches of old Mahmoud, and—the rest is satisfactory."

"Are you sure he killed him?" asked Sterry brutally.

"Killed him? They first unnerved him by the method they learnt of the Algerian spahis, then they tortured him to death slowly—and the devil deserved every pang."

Sterry scowled slightly and looked up at Kell, on whose face was that wide-drawn grin which betokened his complete agreement. They all ate on in silence until Mavis joined them.

"Dr. Shroeder, head of the ambulance corps, insists upon coming over to see you."

"He'll be shot if he does. I can trust 'Foightin' Larry.' Sit down and join us, Mavis. We four are all of the Isocrats now left in Cristallia; we'll have an informal meeting for urgent affairs. Sit down!"

"But he says the wounded are being shamefully neglected."

"Can't help that! Does he suppose that, after all they have done to us, we are going to show any affection for *their* wounded? We are but human."

"Quite right. I am sorry there are any wounded," said Robson.

"We did our best to kill the lot!" And Sterry laughed, and Kell grinned again.

Their cold-hearted callousness surprised her. She could not believe they were in earnest, and turned to her lover and asked pleadingly:

"Won't *you* do anything, Bob?"

He shook his head nonchalantly and wiped his moustache.

"Can't, Mavis. You don't understand these things, or you would know why. Leave them to us and the Kaid Maclean and his Moors. The right thing will be done; you may be sure of that."

"You used not to be like this. What has happened to you all?"

There was no answer.

"Something must be done for them. I will go over myself—that is what Madeline would have done." And she turned away.

"You're right, Mavis; the fighting has made brutes of us all—and I do not wonder at it. You go—we are not fit." And Sterry rose enraged.

Robson muttered something about the usages of war, then took Kell by the arm and walked away.

"Do the best you can for the poor wretches, Mavis.

I will send you all the help we can spare, and Boyd himself will be over on that side soon. There has been harm enough done."

"That is your old good self, Bob," she said, well pleased.

"You would win any one over, Mavis." And putting his arm round her, he drew her to him and kissed her affectionately.

"If only you will do right, the others dare not do wrong."

"With you to win them over to our way—yes." And he kissed her again.

"The future of Cristallia is with you."

"Us," he corrected sharply.

"As you wish, then."

"At last, Mavis."

She bowed her head in acquiescence, and they talked of their own affairs until Jake Hanlan burst in upon them with the news that a runner had come to Kaid Maclean with a message from the Governor of Pieterland surrendering the town and colony to the representatives of the Sultan Abd-el-Azeez of Fez.

"All the same *we* must occupy the place. Where's Kell?"

They found him with Robson, and the two had news of their own to communicate. In the lethal hall they had found the bodies of the two Germans who had stolen the papers from the dead man's desk. So the secret of the destroying "Warstock"—as Redhead named his machine—never left Cristallia after all.

CHAPTER XXX.

CONCLUSION.

TWELVE months have passed since the vibrations of the dreadful "Warstock" in Cristallia shook Europe. Of the many important results which arose from the fruitless expedition against the African Commonwealth none had more far-reaching consequences than the downfall of Germany, for it brought about a European collapse. The terms of the conquerors were hard; but Europe was at their mercy. They insisted upon an indemnity equal to the combined annual naval and military expenditure of the empire for the preceding five years, the payments to extend over a like period, during which time the Cristallians guaranteed Germany against all foreign invasion. Met with the argument that such an arrangement would disturb the balance of power in Europe, they curtly replied that if any State did not agree, one and all would be reduced to the same condition of impotency as the Teutonic Federation. In their wisdom the Governments thought to obtain an advantage by gaining time, but by deferring an attack they allowed the Isocrats to become firmly re-established in the Atlas. In six months' time the chance had gone; the immediate arbiter of the destinies of Europe and Africa was the Chief of the Executive Council in the Cristallian Commonwealth.

Sterry had been elected to that post, and worked hard so to rebuild Cristallia as to surpass all previous achievements. In this he was particularly aided by Iltyd Jones, who, not content with the adoption of his materials for every purpose, was intent upon using them with such originality and effect as to pass the qualifying adjectives "Hildaesque" and "Kewneyesque" from the ranks of artistic slang to the perennial realm of recognised literary currency.

Cristallia itself was greater, richer, and more beautiful than its forerunner. The Capitol was larger, finer, loftier, and on three sides fronted the great north lake, whence issued directly from the water a huge pile of Iltydium, pinnacle on pinnacle, and all gleaming in the sun like the glistening crystals from a frosted icicle. In that way the inventor marked the grave of the two who had been the first to die for the Commonwealth.

There was a fête at Cristallia when the monument was finished, and it served also to celebrate the marriages of Robert Sterry and Iltyd Jones, and the appointment of Boyd Robson and Morven Kell to administer huge tracts of the African Hinterland ceded by Germany.

Sterry had little to tell the gathering, forbearing to open recent wounds. Their chief adversary, Fitzjoy, was out of office, and long likely to remain so. The demands for admission to the colony and the community were more numerous than they could accept. Means to making wealth were showered upon them, and they had now more to fear from friends than enemies, for in England the party in power not only agreed to every proposal made them, but actually imitated their policy by granting inventors the same protective rights as they already acceded to poets. It was little, but, being in the right direction, might attract some slight support from those who otherwise had gone to Cristallia.

As to their future policy, Sterry spoke confidentially if enigmatically. "The greatest of birds is said to bury its head in the sand, thinking thereby that its body is hidden and safe from attack. We think this is foolish. But the wisest of mortals is apt to thrust up his head into the clouds and believe that his body is then beyond harm from the devils on earth. *We* have learnt that this too is foolish. We shall gaze at the stars sometimes, but, even then, the groundlings shall have the impression that we still are kicking—as we mean that they should."

THE END.

www.ingramcontent.com/pod-product-compliance
Lightning Source LLC
Chambersburg PA
CBHW022011220426
43663CB00007B/1042